Longevity Lifest

How to stay healthier and younger for longer

Companion Notebook

Longevity Lifestyle Matters—

How to stay healthier and younger for longer

Companion Notebook

Arlene R. Taylor PhD
with Steve Horton MPH, and Sharlet M. Briggs PhD

Success Resources International, Napa, CA

Longevity Lifestyle Matters—
Companion Notebook

Address requests for information to:

www.LongevityLifestyleMatters.com

ISBN # 1-887307-46-X

Cover picture by Lawrence Smith, www.bylastingimpressions.com

Special thanks to Michelle Nash and Brenda L. Balding

Art Consultation by Seth Foley, www.sfoleystudios.com

Cover design and production by David O. Eastman

Table of Contents

Acknowledgements

Thank you to those who reviewed the manuscript and offered valuable feedback.

Dedication

This *Longevity Lifestyle Matters—Companion Notebook* is dedicated to all individuals who desire to prevent whatever illnesses can be prevented, have embraced the secrets of a Longevity Lifestyle, and purpose to live as long as possible with high levels of mental, physical, emotional, spiritual, and social healthiness. They are choosing to keep their brain, body, and weight in the game!

Publisher's Reminder

This *Longevity Lifestyle Matters—Companion Notebook* is not a medical, psychological, biological, or gerontology textbook. The information and resources herein are for general educational and informational purposes only and do not present an in-depth treatment of specific research findings or topics. The information and program are not intended to take the place of professional counseling, medical or psychological care, recovery therapy, or personalized recommendations from healthcare professionals. Since every brain is different there are no guarantees of individual results.

Be sure to consult your physician, therapist, or other healthcare professionals including registered dieticians and certified exercise physiologists and trainers before you make lifestyle changes or implement new exercise strategies. The publisher, authors, contributors, editors, certified facilitators or volunteers expressly disclaim all responsibility and any liability whatsoever (direct or indirect) for outcomes or adverse effects (actual or perceived), from the use or misuse or inappropriate application of concepts presented herein.

If you find errors or typos in this book, please know that they serve a purpose. Making mistakes is part and parcel of being human—and some brains really enjoy looking for mistakes.

There's no magic bullet. You gotta eat healthy and live healthy to be healthy and look healthy. End of story.

—Morgan Spurlock
Don't Eat This Book

Prologue

The passenger settled into an airplane seat. After take-off, one by one apples, carrot-sticks, celery stalks, and almonds emerged from a carry-on.

"That looks like healthy food," said another traveler who was seated across the aisle.

"I don't find airplane food all that healthy," the first passenger responded, "so I bring my own snacks. This should hold me until we reach Tokyo in seven hours or so."

"You must be a member of Club 122 Longevity," said the other traveler.

"A member of *what*?" The first passenger's eyebrows lifted.

"Club 122 Longevity. You know, people who embrace a Longevity Lifestyle with the goal of living to be at least 122 years old—if not more—with good levels of mental, emotional, physical, and spiritual function. The name actually comes from the longest unambiguously documented human lifespan of a woman in France who lived to be 122 years, 164 days: Jeanne Louise Calment."

"Oh my goodness," said the first passenger. "I'd love to join that club and embrace that goal!"

You can—by creating and maintaining a Longevity Lifestyle. It begins with a positive mindset, a decision to get started, and the use of willpower to help you follow through on your goals.

> *Being positive doesn't necessarily come naturally. We have to make that decision daily.*
>
> —Joel Olsteen

This *Companion Notebook* is designed to help you refocus the information you learned from your reading of *Lifestyle Longevity Matters—Keeping Your Brain, Body, and Weight in the Game*, turn it into knowledge, personalize that knowledge, and practically apply it in ways that work for your brain and body.

After all, you *do* want to go beyond just reading about a Longevity Lifestyle. You want to actually create one that will work for you now and for the rest of your life. *Taste* the fruits of your knowledge, if you will, and discover how good a Longevity Lifestyle can be.

For the optimum benefit, take a few minutes each day to go through the pages that correlate with the specific week, complete the reading assignment, and refer to the Selected Bibliography in *Longevity Lifestyle Matters—Keeping Your Brain and Body in the Game* for additional resources. Take time to write down your goals, thoughts, and choices.

You are encouraged to read aloud from both *Longevity Lifestyle Matters* and the *Companion Notebook.*

> *Did you know that reading aloud is an anti-aging strategy? Read aloud for at least ten minutes a day because reading aloud is a challenging exercise for the brain. When you read aloud you see, hear, and articulate the words, which help move them into long-term memory.*

As you become enthusiastic with the progress you are making—from feeling better, looking better, thinking better, role-modeling better, and realizing more energy to accomplish some of your cherished goals—let your actions and behaviors speak for you. Answer questions as you choose but avoid grabbing others by the ear and telling them what you think they should do in their life. The 2nd Century Greek Philosopher, Epictetus, might have had experiences along this line. Something prompted his suggestion.

> *Preach not to others what they should eat, but eat as becomes you—and be silent.*
>
> —Epictetus

Think of this *Companion Notebook* as a record of the first twelve weeks of your Longevity Lifestyle journey. Refer to it often and remind yourself what you are accomplishing. Use the note sections to chronicle your successes and anecdotes to review periodically.

In case you're wondering the reason you should go to the trouble of actually writing down your responses to the exercises, Michael O'Brien and Larry Shook point out that as you answer the questions, *Journaling takes away the wiggle room you can leave yourself.*

Sure you can just read the questions and not do the exercises, but that is a sure fire way not to profit from experience by wiggling away from the denial and from the sometimes uncomfortable insights and lessons that tough issues bring. In order to keep your brain, body and weight in the game for actual growth and development, you'll need to incorporate the new patterns into your life in a disciplined way. Picture in your mind's eye where you are starting and where you are heading. Review your internal mental picture (map) every morning and whenever you have the urge to deviate from your chosen path. And on those times when at least one foot slips off the track, pull it up and deliberately place it back on your Longevity Lifestyle journey.

Always bear in mind that your own resolution to succeed is more important than any one thing.

—Abraham Lincoln

After the first twelve weeks (the recommendation is to do one Section each week), go through this *Companion Notebook* again, and again—least once a year. The more times you review the information, the more likely you are to embrace it and live it. Be serious about your Longevity Lifestyle, but avoid overreacting about every little (or big!) thing that happens along the way.

The appendix in this *Companion Notebook* contains:

- Comparison Measurement forms so you can keep track of your BMI, waist measurement, and weight on a weekly basis

- Daily Points forms so you can track and stay motivated with the important daily strategies you are implementing

- Track Your Intake and Analyze Your Intake forms, a proven strategy for helping you manage your menu choices and intake more successfully

- Additional examples of foods with their position on the Glycemic Index and Glycemic Load lists

- Sample recipes. Personalize them to work for you. The practice will help you gain skills for preparing healthier dishes than some you may have been accustomed to in the past. More recipes are available at:

www.LongevityLifestyleMatters.com

And as you are making this Longevity Lifestyle journey a success, remember to laugh. A lot. An old proverb says: Laugh and last. Laughter is the elixir of life that makes almost everything 'taste' better. Emerging research is revealing how beneficial mirthful laughter is to both brain and body. Some have suggested that human beings need a minimum of thirty mirthful laughs per day. People who are considered to be very happy—and who, incidentally, are often both healthy and long lived, as well—reportedly laugh between 100 and 400 times a day. Do you need to include more laughter in your daily life? If so, do whatever it takes to achieve that.

> *A cheerful heart is good like medicine.*
>
> —Proverbs 17:22

One last thing: be kind to yourself in doing the *Companion Notebook.* If you feel resistant to some of the items included—or even intimidated—know that can be a signal that whatever that item is, it holds special value to you. Ask yourself where you got that special value. Proceed with patience and kindness. Analyze honestly. That item of special value may be something you want to retain; it may be something that would be beneficial to alter in some way.

In a time of drastic change it is the learners who inherit the future. The learned usually find themselves equipped to live in a world that no longer exists.

—Eric Hoffer

So this is where rubber meets the road to begin creating and practically applying strategies that align with a Longevity Lifestyle. Strategies that you will maintain for as long as you live. You can't do anything about the past. You can create a healthier future for yourself.

> *The best way to predict the future is to create it.*
>
> —Abraham Lincoln

Create a healthier future for yourself.

Savor the promise, the experience, the rewards, and the success. Know that you can do it!

—The Authors

My Starting Data

Body Mass Index (BMI) Calculation

Calculate your BMI using a BMI Calculator, available at:

www.LongevityLifestyleMatters.com
Information – Drop-down menu

Data Recording

Record your initial data using US or metric.

BMI: 26

Check the appropriate category below

- ☐ Underweight = BMI below 18.5
- ☐ Normal weight = BMI between 18.5–24.9
- ☑ Overweight = BMI between 25–29.9
- ☐ Obesity = BMI of 30 or greater

Height: 5 ft. 8 in. or ________ cm

Waist measurement: 38 in. or ________ cm

Weight: 172 pounds or _______ Kg

Also record your data on page 121 of the Appendix for ongoing comparison.

Replacement Concept

On a daily basis, deliberately choose to replace at least one unhealthy food or beverage with one that is healthier. For example:

Replace ____________________________ with ____________________________

Replace ____________________________ with ____________________________

It isn't where you came from—

it's where you're going

that counts.

—Ella Fitzgerald

Welcome to Section 1

Record your measurements in the Appendix

Perhaps you have heard that the be-all, end-all, and cure-all for weight management is a low-carbohydrate diet. Avoid jumping on that bandwagon. Carbs provide vital fuel—glucose—for your brain, body, and muscles. And according to some physicians, healthier carbs are the preferred type of fuel, especially for the brain and nervous system. Current recommendations are that half to two-thirds of your daily caloric intake need to be in the form of carbohydrates. Avoid sugar; white rice and white flour; and refined and processed foods made with them. Instead, select healthier whole-food carbs and eat them in as natural a state as possible.

Read Foreword, Prologue, and Chapters 1-2

Checking-In

Circle the number on the scale below that represents your level of interest in creating and maintaining a brain-based Longevity Lifestyle.
Scale: 1 = low and 5 = high.

1-----2-----3-----4-----5 (4 circled)

Name your #1 motivator for creating and maintaining a Longevity Lifestyle.

So I can experience the best over-all health possible!

Circle the number on the scale below that represents your level of knowledge about the factors research indicates impact your brain-body health and potential longevity. Scale: 1 = low and 5 = high. **1-----2-----3-----4-----5** (4 circled)

Take your picture

Stand in front of a mirror in minimal clothing and take a picture. Next, turn to the side and take a picture of your profile. You might like what you see—or not. You need not show it to anyone. Just take the pictures. Wait until the 12th Section to take the next picture. It's difficult to notice changes on a day-to-day basis. Photos can help you see how your body is transitioning.

Ground Rule: Measure and weigh ***WEEKLY*** only. Your body is an incredibly complex complication of biochemical machinery with continual hormonal and chemical fluctuations. Your weight can vary by several pounds over the course of a day. Daily weighing and measuring can promote an unhealthy perspective where every tiny change may be scrutinized and blown out of proportion. This can sabotage your overall success. Be wise. Measure weekly ***only***.

Prologue

Reinforcing what you learn

Collective wisdom highlights the importance of taking personal responsibility for your own brain and body. In the past, which of these have you tried?

- ❒ Miracle pills
- ❒ Bingeing and purging
- ❒ Liquid diets
- ❒ Injections
- ☑ Prepared pre-purchased meals
- ☑ Exercise equipment
- ❒ *Magic* or other quick-fix promises
- ❒ Other ______________________

Scientists generally recognize five main determinants of health that can impact disease and longevity. There are others, as well. Check any of the following that you believe has hindered you in your journey toward health and longevity:

- ❒ Genetics and epigenetics
- ☑ Individual choices/behaviors
- ❒ Social environments
- ❒ Physical environments
- ❒ Access to health services
- ☑ Personal laziness
- ❒ Expectations of self/others
- ☑ Lack of good self-care
- ❒ Addictive behaviors
- ❒ Influence of friends/family
- ❒ Lack of knowledge
- ❒ Birth defects
- ☑ Failure to delay gratification
- ❒ Other ______________

How are you addressing these so you stay *in the game* you were 'meant to play'?

Remembering that it is in me to make the necessary changes, I can do it.

Those who want something very badly, find a way.
Those who don't, find an excuse.
—Anonymous

Where Rubber Meets the Road

Reinforcing what you learn

Blue Zone people in several different parts of the globe tend to live significantly longer than most others. Their style of living tends to sound a lot like a Longevity Lifestyle.

Check any of the following that are *currently* part of your lifestyle.

- [ ] PAC mindset
- [ ] Optimum sleep on a daily basis
- [ ] Appropriate hydration with water
- [ ] Brain protection strategies
- [x] Physical activity and exercise
- [ ] Challenging brain stimulation
- [x] Exposure to natural light
- [ ] Healthy nutrition eating style
- [ ] Pesco-vegetarian eating style
- [x] Vegetarian or vegan style of eating
- [ ] Laughter and play
- [ ] Support network
- [ ] Positive self-talk style
- [ ] Balanced work-home life
- [ ] Stress Management
- [ ] High Emotional Intelligence
- [ ] Life satisfaction
- [ ] Fast, fatty, fried, frozen foods
- [ ] Sodas, sugary drinks, juices
- [ ] Regular meals/portion control
- [ ] Frequent snacking
- [x] Desserts on a regular basis
- [ ] Beer, Wine, or Spritzers
- [ ] Tobacco in any form
- [ ] Mind-altering drugs
- [ ] Other ____________________

List ONE new key point you learned in Chapter 1.

most of what I need to change in my control.

All about You

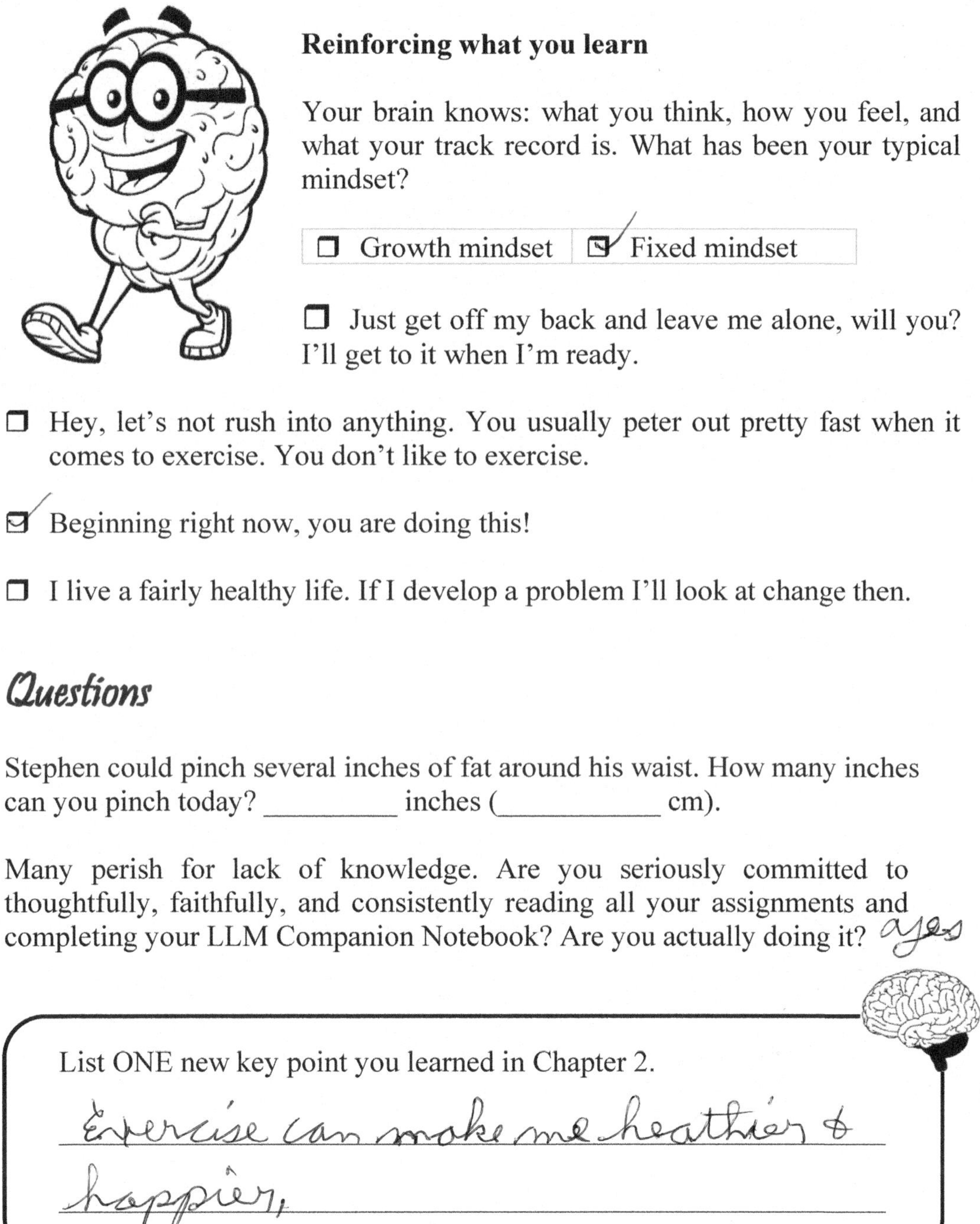

Reinforcing what you learn

Your brain knows: what you think, how you feel, and what your track record is. What has been your typical mindset?

☐ Growth mindset	☑ Fixed mindset

☐ Just get off my back and leave me alone, will you? I'll get to it when I'm ready.

☐ Hey, let's not rush into anything. You usually peter out pretty fast when it comes to exercise. You don't like to exercise.

☑ Beginning right now, you are doing this!

☐ I live a fairly healthy life. If I develop a problem I'll look at change then.

Questions

Stephen could pinch several inches of fat around his waist. How many inches can you pinch today? _________ inches (___________ cm).

Many perish for lack of knowledge. Are you seriously committed to thoughtfully, faithfully, and consistently reading all your assignments and completing your LLM Companion Notebook? Are you actually doing it? yes

List ONE new key point you learned in Chapter 2.

Exercise can make me heathier & happier.

My Personal Commitment

Even if you're on the right track, you'll get run over if you just sit there.
—Will Rogers

If you can imagine it, you can achieve it. If you can dream it, you can become it.
—William Arthur Ward

Identify anything that is holding you back. Bad habit of putting things off till tomorrow.

Are you ready to keep you brain, body, and weight in the game? Take the first step. Make a personal commitment for a Longevity Lifestyle now!

☑ (Your name) James, you are doing everything within your power to learn information about the brain, health, and longevity. You are embracing a Longevity Lifestyle—one that you are creating and maintaining for the rest of your life. You are practically applying the strategies on a daily basis, and are committed to *do* what you *know* for as long as you live! You realize you are the only person who can do this for you.

Remember: be sure to consult your healthcare professionals before beginning an exercise program—especially if you have not been exercising regularly.

Use it—or lose it!
—Jimmy Connors

Move it—or lose it!
—Pierce J. Howard PhD

Access the resources found at:

www.LongevityLifestyleMatters.com

www.SharletBriggs.com

www.ArleneTaylor.org

Gifts for Yourself and Others

Your brain can only do what it thinks it can do—your mindset, thoughts, and self-talk tell your brain what it can do

If you think you can or you think you can't—you are right! It's not always that you do not know what to do—rather it's often that you do not do what you know. Break that unhelpful cycle. Alter your mindset. Take charge of your self-talk. Others are doing this. So can ***you***. This is how to succeed:

- Study and learn so you know what to do.
- Turn the information you learn in knowledge.
- Practically apply your knowledge. Really ***do*** what you ***know***.
- Tell your brain what it can do and that you expect it to help you.
- Use willpower to follow through and keep on keeping on. & God's help
- Thank your brain for helping you ***do*** what you ***know.***
- Create and maintain a Longevity Lifestyle for as long as you live.
- Aim high. You'll likely get much farther.
- Stay mindfully aware and be consistent.
- Laugh, have fun, and enjoy the journey—it goes by quickly!

Thinking Ahead

Name two individuals who also are likely to benefit from the gift of a Longevity Lifestyle that you are giving yourself:

1. ______________________________ 2. ______________________________

Living Younger Longer

You are getting to do what many others never had the opportunity to do—and what still others will never get the opportunity to do. What good fortune for you!

You glance in the mirror and realize that things have shifted a bit. It's easy to concentrate on thinning hair, wrinkles, gradual loss of some strength and flexibility, a need for glasses, the fact that your chest wants to get better acquainted with your waist, and so on. Stop whining, complaining, blaming, and making excuses. A Longevity Lifestyle recommends that you create a 'growth' mindset and be grateful for the opportunity to be alive and to continue living. And smile, for heaven's sake. It's an instant face lift…

Rather than wishing things were different, be grateful that research is showing you how to live younger longer. Appreciate the fact that Jeanne Louise Calment—a life-long resident of Arles in Southern France who lived to be 122 years 164 days—demonstrated that living longer and keeping life and energy and satisfaction in your years is doable.

Thank your brain for helping you reach your present age—you are fortunate to be alive—and list two things for which you are clearly grateful:

1. I can still change my bad habits.
2. God will help me do it.

Use Your Neurons! Come on—you can do it!

Calculate how much dirt in cubic feet there is in a hole that measures three by four feet and five feet deep.

My Notes

(Your name) James**, you are remembering this:**

(1.) avoid sugar, white rice & flour, and the refined & processed foods made with them. (2.) Weigh self Wednesday morning after urinating, also figure BMI & record. (3.) Read notes from notebook each morning to remind self, what I am making part of my longevity lifestyle.

You've got to win in your

mind before you win

in your life.

—John Addison

Welcome to Section 2

Record your measurements
in the Appendix

Have you been led to believe that *carbohydrates are the enemy?* Not so fast! Some of them are but avoid taring and feathering all carbs simply because an apple barrel contains some bad apples, so to speak. That would be like throwing out the baby with the bath water—never recommended. Science supports the use of these carbs for weight loss and overall health. Some physicians point out that carbohydrates are the best source of fuel for your brain—high quality carbs, of course, because they're not all created equal. Just like calories and cars and cell phones are not all created equal. The three categories of carbs—simple, complex, and fiber—each contain some high-quality healthier carbs. Eat them in as natural state as possible.

Read Chapters 3-4 and
Longevity Lifestyle Components

Checking-In

Even if you're not fully ready to face your body image head on or identify factors that contributed to your weighing too little or too much, becoming aware of the challenges you're facing is critical. Take a moment to identify the challenges you faced during the past few days.

Name three of your challenges:

1. ______________________________

2. ______________________________

3. ______________________________

Were your challenges: ❒ Actual ❒ Virtual ❒ Real ❒ Resolvable

❒ Imagined ❒ Serious ❒ Piddling ❒ Unresolvable

How did you deal with those challenges? ______________________________

____

How effective were your strategies? ______________________________

____

How are you tweaking them to make them more effective? ______________________________

____

Diving Deeper

If you're new to a Longevity Lifestyle (and even if you're not), you may think that a successful journey is one that's struggle-free. Think again. Success starts the day you snap out of your old habits and begin thinking, talking, eating, and exercising differently. And you get more and more successful each day that you keep your brain, body, and weight in the game. You may not do it in the best possible style every day. Getting thrown off track occasionally does not mean you've messed up for good. Set yourself up for success, knowing there will be ups and downs. Understand that and you're ahead of most people on this planet and well on your way to lifelong success.

What did you do well during the past few days? ______________________

____

____

Looking forward, what will you do differently? ______________________

____

____

If you stubbed your toe, stepped on the nail of an old habit, slipped off the path, overindulged, or lapsed completely in terms of your daily goals, avoid beating yourself up. Learn the lesson. Let go of shame or it may tempt you to stop tracking what you eat or quit exercising all together. STOP going there. Filling out your Daily Points form can keep you consciously and mindfully aware of what you're actually doing. You can use it—together with this *Companion Notebook*—to monitor your actions and behaviors and, most importantly, evaluate the reason you're getting the results that you are getting. Remember, this is a brain-based journey. You and your brain. Together. A powerful combination!

PAC for Success

Reinforcing what you learn

Tell your brain now:

(Your first name) __________, you are . . .

Write beside each letter in the PAC acronym below what you are telling your brain—the specific actions it can take to help you and what each behavior looks like.

P ____

____

A ____

____

C ____

____

you're going nowhere without it.
If your brain is your vehicle to success, then your fuel is self-motivation. No matter how intelligent you are,
—Melchor Lim

List ONE new key point you learned in Chapter 3.

____

____

Eavesdropping on the Brain

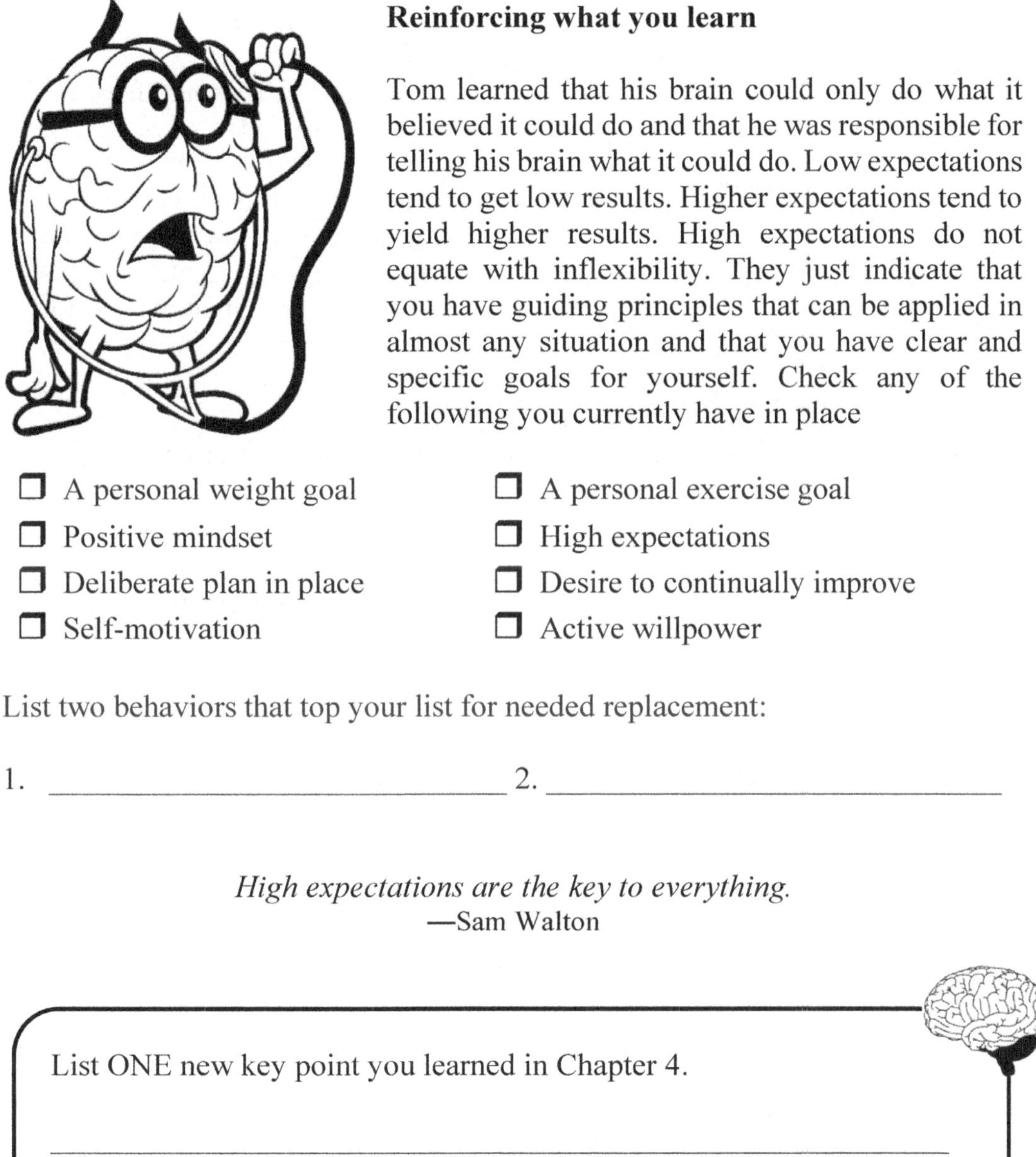

Reinforcing what you learn

Tom learned that his brain could only do what it believed it could do and that he was responsible for telling his brain what it could do. Low expectations tend to get low results. Higher expectations tend to yield higher results. High expectations do not equate with inflexibility. They just indicate that you have guiding principles that can be applied in almost any situation and that you have clear and specific goals for yourself. Check any of the following you currently have in place

- ❒ A personal weight goal
- ❒ Positive mindset
- ❒ Deliberate plan in place
- ❒ Self-motivation
- ❒ A personal exercise goal
- ❒ High expectations
- ❒ Desire to continually improve
- ❒ Active willpower

List two behaviors that top your list for needed replacement:

1. ____________________________ 2. ____________________________

High expectations are the key to everything.
—Sam Walton

List ONE new key point you learned in Chapter 4.

____

____

Appendix - Longevity Lifestyle Components

Reinforcing what you learn

Most people replicate either what they saw role-modeled in childhood or swing 180 degrees opposite. However, 180 degrees from dysfunctional is still dysfunctional. A few take the good things with them, let go what was undesirable, and create a brain-based Longevity Lifestyle that works for them, maintaining it for as long as they live.

What type of lifestyle did you see role-modeling growing up? Describe it.

____

What type of lifestyle do you want for the rest of your life? Describe it.

____

Ability is what you're capable of doing. Motivation determines what you do. Attitude determines how well you do it.
—Lou Holtz

If it came from a plant, eat it; if it was made in a 'plant,' don't.
—Michael Pollan

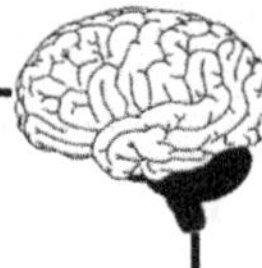

List ONE new key point you learned while reviewing the basic Longevity Lifestyle Components in the Appendix.

____

____

Give Gifts to Yourself and Others

Get your weight and BMI into the 'normal' range and keep them there—give your brain a break today and for the rests of your life!

A study in the journal Neurobiology of Aging reported that a higher BMI was associated with shrinkage in every region of the cerebral cortex.

Tufts University reported on a ten-year study of 6,401 British civil servants that found an association between being overweight or obese and impaired cognitive function. When this was combined with metabolic abnormalities, (diabetes, high cholesterol) the odds of mental decline increased over time. Those with a higher BMI, were significantly more likely to show a faster rate of cognitive decline over a ten-year period. Even in metabolically healthy individuals, a higher BMI was associated with poorer cognitive function.

Studies of 8,000 sets of twins showed that being overweight ***doubled*** the risk of dementia, while being obese ***quadrupled*** the risk. Ouch!

Where are you right now in terms of your weight-related risk for dementia?

❐ Normal ❐ Overweight ❐ Obese ❐ Morbidly obese

Thinking Ahead

List two individuals who would benefit from the gift you are giving yourself of your weight and BMI into the 'normal' range and keeping them there:

1. ______________________________ 2. ______________________________

Living Younger Longer

You have more time to recognize and internalize that age is just a number—a matter of the mind—and if you don't mind, it doesn't matter

You are a combination of at least three different types of *ages* (and there may be others, as well, such as your emotional intelligence age or your social age):

1. Your chronological age, which cannot be changed. You can lie about it, of course, but lying is believed to suppress immune system function and you want to avoid that! A Longevity Lifestyle may help you keep life in your years and maybe even extend them. It's worth a shot.

2. Your psychological age, which can be changed. You know people who seem much older than their chronological age and others who seem much younger and who are interested in everything.

3. Your biological age, which can be speeded up or slowed down. One goal of a Longevity Lifestyle is to slow down one's biological age and retard the onset of symptoms of aging insofar as it is possible to do so.

How old would you think your age was if you didn't know your chronological age? What do you guesstimate your psychological and biological ages to be?

Chronological age ____ Psychological age ____ Biological age ____

Use Your Neurons! Come on—you can do it!

Prior to the discovery and naming of Mt. Everest, what mountain had the highest elevation above sea level on planet earth?

My Notes

(Your name) ________, you are remembering this:

____

____

____

____

____

____

____

____

____

____

The big secret in life is that there is no big secret. Whatever your goal, you can get there if you're willing to work.

—Oprah Winfrey

Welcome to Section 3

Record your measurements in the Appendix

How did carbs get such a bad rap? It likely started when big industry began 'refining' them, removing many healthy ingredients, and turning them into processed food on a grand scale. Metaphorically, a similar thing happened when Yellowstone National Park 'refined' its environment and kicked out the coyotes. Fortunately, the pendulum is swinging back toward the middle in much the same way that the Yellowstone National Park environment is being revitalized—now that the coyotes are back. Current recommendations are that half to two-thirds of your daily caloric intake needs to be in the form of high-quality healthier carbs to ensure a sufficient supply for your brain and body.

Read Chapters 5, 6, and 7

Checking-In

Positive self-talk is critical to your success. One day you're breezing through your Longevity Lifestyle and the next day you hit a wall. You may be irritated, tired, angry, detached, fearful, sad or even depressed, to name just a few. Pay attention to your self-talk. What have you been saying to your brain? Be honest!

How many times during any given day do you judge or second-guess yourself?

- ❒ None or extremely rarely
- ❒ 1-2 times per day
- ❒ 3-6 times per day
- ❒ 7-10 times per day
- ❒ Constantly or extremely frequently
- ❒ Other ___________________________

How many times during any given day do you think or say negative things about yourself?

- ❒ None or vary rarely
- ❒ 1-2 times per day
- ❒ 3-6 times per day
- ❒ 7-10 times per day
- ❒ Constantly or very frequently
- ❒ Other ___________________________

To whom have you given permission to trigger negative self-talk in your life?

- ❒ Self
- ❒ Children
- ❒ Boss
- ❒ Friend
- ❒ Spouse or partner
- ❒ Parents
- ❒ Co-Worker or colleague
- ❒ Other_______________________

You can only manage what you can identify and describe. Dig to discover the reason you would allow yourself or anyone else to trigger negative self-talk.

____

Diving Deeper

When you crave food or beverage, pause and become mindfully aware of what is going on in your brain. Perhaps you are feeling angry, anxious, fearful, sad, or excited. Maybe you are actually thirsty and not physiologically hungry. What can your brain adopt to avoid following through on the craving?

- ❏ Go for a walk
- ❏ Drink a glass of water
- ❏ Wait 15 minutes
- ❏ Breathe deeply
- ❏ Think of something else
- ❏ Side track yourself
- ❏ Eat at regular times
- ❏ Call a friend
- ❏ Other ______________

What thoughts or beliefs are you holding onto that are holding you back?

____

____

How many hours of sleep do you routinely get at night? Be honest!

❏ Less than 5 ❏ 5-6 ❏ 6-7 ❏ 7-8 ❏ 8-9 ❏ More than 9

If you sleep less than six hours in twenty-four (and your brain needs more), what is preventing you from getting the sleep your brain needs in order to thrive?

- ❏ Old habits
- ❏ Low self-worth
- ❏ Too much TV
- ❏ Poor Priorities
- ❏ Proving something
- ❏ Avoiding something
- ❏ Unrealistic expectations
- ❏ Escaping from reality
- ❏ Other (write in below)

____

____

White Bear Phenomenon

Reinforcing what you learn

David learned that the subconscious mind follows the pictures created by the conscious mind from your thoughts and words and usually does its best to push you toward those pictures. Once you can identify what your subconscious is telling you, half the battle is won. Make a list of three issues that you consider (or have been told) are 'sore spots' for you.

Sore Spot 1. ____

Sore Spot 2. ____

Sore Spot 3.____

Link an experience in your past with each sore spot and then raise your emotional intelligence to heal those sore spots. What was the lesson or gift?

1. ____

2. ____

3. ____

List ONE new key point you learned in Chapter 5.

____

____

Besotted Brain

Reinforcing what you learn

Everyone has some type of self-medication patterns but not everyone identifies them. The wellness coach asked Josh to take a long hard look at his habit patterns around self-medication.

What are your eating and/or drinking habit patterns around self-medication?

- ❒ Salty taste
- ❒ Chicken
- ❒ Cookies
- ❒ Meat
- ❒ Cheese
- ❒ Chocolate
- ❒ Ice Cream
- ❒ French Fries
- ❒ Dairy dips
- ❒ Cake or pies
- ❒ Sweet taste
- ❒ Pasta
- ❒ Pizza
- ❒ Chips, crackers
- ❒ Bacon
- ❒ Burgers
- ❒ Sodas or colas
- ❒ Bread
- ❒ Bacon 'n eggs
- ❒ Excess eating
- ❒ Crunchy taste
- ❒ Soft 'ice cream'
- ❒ Smooth taste
- ❒ Caffeinated drinks
- ❒ Wine, beer, spritzers
- ❒ Mac 'n cheese
- ❒ Potato anything
- ❒ Buttered popcorn
- ❒ Pancakes or waffles
- ❒ Other ___________

List ONE new key point you learned in Chapter 6.

____

____

Slow and Steady Wins

Reinforcing what you learn

Alba learned that food restrictions (deprivation) can lead to bingeing. What is your history related to restricting foods or deprivation and bingeing?

❒ None ❒ Rare

❒ Periodic ❒ Often

What triggers the deprivation and/or bingeing? ______________________

____

____

Your plan for breaking this cycle and start date? ______________________

____

Do you need to ask someone to help hold you accountable based on your track-record of holding yourself accountable and if so, who?

____

List ONE new key point you learned in Chapter 7.

____

____

Gifts for Yourself and Others

Practice giving your brain choices on a regular basis—only two at a time because your brain only has two hemispheres. Make your decisions based on the potential long-term impact and negative or positive outcome to your life. Then use willpower to implement your decisions.

Willpower is a function of the prefrontal cortex, located directly behind your forehead. This part of the brain matures slowly and may be developed by the mid to late twenties. Until then, hopefully you regularly have practiced using willpower and developed good habits as your brain matured. Willpower rarely works well to deprive yourself of something you already do for gratification (e.g., ending a habit that gives you a momentary reward but a long-term negative outcome such as over-eating or too little moving). Willpower is designed to give you energetic perseverance to attain a goal and to:

- Develop a brand NEW behavior
- Create a healthier REPLACEMENT behavior

Although willpower was not designed to stop a behavior that is already giving you some type of *reward*—and rarely works well for that—it can help you maintain a brain-based Longevity Lifestyle that involves developing and implementing new or healthier replacement behaviors. After all, you taught your brain to recognize a reward—you can teach it to recognize a new reward.

Thinking Ahead

Who in your life would benefit from your role-modeling the gift of willpower?

____

Living Younger Longer

Due to the gift of more time, you have the opportunity to continue honing your intelligent or creative memory, which can strengthen with age. Put your time, energy, and money on strategies that can help strengthen this type of memory

Declarative or verbal memory (you know facts and can state them) gradually can tend to weaken with age.

Non-declarative or nonverbal memory (you know how to do things such as ride a bicycle or play a musical instrument but you cannot state exactly how it happens) also can gradually weaken with age.

Intelligent or creative memory is composed of three elements:

- Memory pieces—information (data, facts) you have learned, knowledge you have gained, and what you've gleaned through personal experience

- Connections and associations among those memory pieces—the more you've made the more likely you are to recall and reassemble them

- The distinctive mental processing that occurs through mixing and matching pieces and connections—which can provide insight, help with problem-solving, enhance creativity, and help to keep your brain sharp

Do something every day to hone your intelligent or creative memory.

Use Your Neurons! Come on—you can do it!

In France you cannot take a picture of an individual with a wooden leg.
Do you know the reason?

My Notes

(Your name) ________, you are remembering this:

First say to yourself what you

would be—then do what

you have to do.

—Epictetus
2nd Century Greek Philosopher

Welcome to Section 4

Record your measurements
in the Appendix

According to Elisa Zied RD: "Carbs are *not* the enemy." The enemy is often a lack of information or a failure to turn what you learn into knowledge and practically apply it on a daily basis. An all-or-nothing approach to carbohydrates is like avoiding all dogs simply because some bite. Yes, some dogs are vicious and yes, some carbs are unhealthy. Dropping unwanted pounds and then maintaining your weight within a more optimum range typically requires you to reduce your intake of poor quality refined and processed carbs and increase your intake of healthier unrefined carbs. Your brain, nervous system, and muscles need them. Develop a balanced approach to quality nutrition and a Longevity Lifestyle.

Read Chapters 8-9 and 12 Steps of a Longevity Lifestyle

Checking-In

If your reason for not adopting a Longevity Lifestyle is that you think you don't have enough time: decide to do it. Picture it in your mind's eye, access willpower to implement what you visualize—and it'll be more likely to happen. List four things that went easier during these past few days.

1. ______________________________

2. ______________________________

3. ______________________________

4. ______________________________

Stories abound of individuals suffering a severe trauma, like a heart attack or stroke or cancer, and how that life event led to a permanent change in their lifestyle habits.

Avoid waiting for something traumatic to happen to you in order to get motivated. Your willpower is within you. Identify healthier replacement behaviors and engage your willpower to help you reach your goals!

No matter how you choose to approach a Longevity Lifestyle, it's important to take small steps and set small manageable goals. Remain in good spirits. Trying to do too much too fast can set you up for failure. Be happy with small steps and small manageable goals, be consistent, and you will see results far more quickly. What's more, you'll have a much higher probability of turning those gains into life-long habits.

Diving Deeper

You have a brain-body connection—the interaction among three factors: the functioning of your brain, your mindset, and your physical health. Scientists are becoming convinced that length of life depends on a dynamic interplay of these three factors. This isn't mind over matter. It is mind and matter in collaboration. Learning about your brain and applying that knowledge on a daily basis, can positively impact your life. Remember, seventy percent of how well and how long you live is in your hands. Which of the following are already in your hands?

- ❐ An optimally functioning brain
- ❐ A healthy immune system
- ❐ A sound body
- ❐ A positive mindset and self-talk patterns
- ❐ A supportive social network
- ❐ An implemented plan for financial security

What are your plans to take advantage of the potential opportunity to live younger for longer?

____

____

____

Death by Sitting

Reinforcing what you learn

When Marie learned the importance of physical movement and activity, she stated she was committed to increasing her level of exercise. Physical activity and exercise are critical for a Longevity Lifestyle. Scientists haven't figured out exactly how much a specific person needs but everyone agrees that appropriate physical activity and exercise are healthful while inactivity is not. In fact, low physical activity is a powerful predictor of early mortality.

What did you see role-modeled about exercise during childhood?

What is your exercise strategy in adulthood?

To start strengthing exercise next week

If it's not already in place, what is your target date? 6/11/23

List ONE new key point you learned in Chapter 8.

Walk six days a week

Booting up Your Brain

Reinforcing what you learn

Marge learned that regular physical activity and physical exercise helps many of the body's systems function better, keeps heart disease, diabetes type 2, and a host of other diseases at bay, and is key for maintaining optimum weight. Have you been successful at engaging in regular physical activity and physical exercise? If not, make a date with yourself—and craft a plan.

What exercise type(s) have you selected?

___

Where are you exercising?

___

When are you exercising and for how many minutes at a time?

___

How many total minutes per week are you exercising? ___

What are you doing to make it fun? ___

List ONE new key point you learned in Chapter 9.

1. Eat 2 servings of vegetables/day, 1 raw if possible. 2. Eat at least 1 fresh fruit/day.

Twelve Steps of a Longevity Lifestyle

Reinforcing what you learn

The Twelve Steps of a Longevity Lifestyle are basic and simple. You simply make sure your mindset and self-talk are on board. Then you decide how to implement each component in your everyday routine in a way that works for your brain. Next, pick one, choose to do it, and activate willpower to help you follow through. As soon as that component is in place, select another, and then another, and so on. Before long you'll have created and implemented a brain-based Longevity Lifestyle. Then you just keep on keeping on. How many of the twelve steps are you already doing on a regular basis?

- ❐ Step 1
- ❐ Step 2
- ❐ Step 3
- ❐ Step 4
- ❐ Step 5
- ❐ Step 6
- ❐ Step 7
- ❐ Step 8
- ❐ Step 9
- ❐ Step 10
- ❐ Step 11
- ❐ Step 12

List ONE new key point you learned in reviewing the Twelve Steps of a Longevity Lifestyle in the Appendix.

____

____

Gifts for Yourself and Others

Behaviors that result in undesirable outcomes do not occur in a vacuum. Be very clear—every pathology has an ecology, an environment that allows it to thrive. Stop creating an environment that allows pathology to thrive

You are where you are today because of the choices you made in the past. Likewise, in the future you will be where you are because of the choices you make today, tomorrow, and the next day. Habits are simply choices you make on a regular basis, often automatically or semi-automatically. Typically they are an attempt at *self-medication*—doing something to make yourself feel better in the immediate moment with little or no thought about the future and the potential result down the line.

All human beings self-medicate—but the way in which they do this differs dramatically. You can self-medicate directly with food, beverages, medications, or drugs and indirectly by what you read, watch, and do, along with activities such as mental and physical exercise, sex, risk-taking, social media, technology, and even strong emotions you hang onto. Additive behaviors are simply self-medicating choices that have run away with themselves. Positive self-medication activities result in positive outcomes; negative self-medication activities result in negative outcomes. Give yourself the gift of making choices that result in positive outcomes, which typically leave much less to *clean up*.

Thinking Ahead

Name two individuals who would welcome your decision to make choices that result in positive outcomes:

1. ______________________________ 2. ______________________________

Living Younger Longer

You are learning that prevention is better than cure. You have learned some helpful strategies related to growing older more gracefully. You understand the importance of applying these strategies on a daily basis and are using willpower to follow through

Benign Senescence is a term for age-related forgetfulness, some of which is preventable. Tell yourself every day: "(First name ______, you are retaining your memory."

- Read aloud for at least ten minutes a day. Engage in challenging and stimulating brain activities for at least thirty minutes a day.
- Build your vocabulary. While mental nimbleness for accessing words instantly can decline with age, your vocabulary can improve.
- Take a class at the local Junior College. Research in three countries has shown that for every year of education beyond basic college (or its equivalent) you may reduce your risk of Alzheimer's by twenty percent.
- Play, laugh, and have fun. Fill your life with healthy pleasures.

Use Your Neurons! Come on—you can do it!

Aoccdrnig to rscheraeres at Cmabrgide Uinervtisy, it deosn't mtetar in waht oredr the ltteers in a wrod are witretn, the olny iprmoatnt tihng is taht the frist and lsat ltteer of each word be in the rghit pclae. The rset can be a taotl mses and you can siltl raed it wouthit a porbelm. Tihs is bcuseae yuor huamn biarn deos not raed ervey lteter by istlef, but the wrod as a wlohe. Amzanig huh? I cdnuolt blveiee taht I cluod aulaclty uesdnatnrd waht I was rdanieg. It's just the phaonmneal pweor of the hmuan mnid!

My Notes

(Your name) _______, you are remembering this:

If we could give every individual the right amount of nourishment and exercise, not too little and not too much, we would have found the safest way to health.

—Hippocrates

Welcome to Section 5

Record your measurements in the Appendix

Your body is a complex and world-class organization. Its primary source of energy is carbohydrates that it breaks down into glucose, which forms the fuel your brain, central nervous system, red-blood cells, and muscles require, to name just a few. Limiting carbs too severely or for too long a period of time is unwise and may force the body to steal from muscles or other body organs or try to use proteins and fats in an attempt to find fuel to power its many functions. There is even concern about the potential long-term impact on brain function that may result from a failure to give it sufficient amounts of high quality healthier carbs on a regular basis.

Read Chapters 10-12

Checking-In

Everyone absorbs some stereotypical beliefs, although not all identify them. For example, 'People always look worse as they get older.' Or 'It's inevitable. Soon you won't know a cabbage from a computer.' Or 'You're way too old to learn how to do an Internet search.'

Your self-identified stereotypically absorbed beliefs and self-talk style play key roles toward failure or success.

Identify two stereotypical beliefs

1 ____

2 ____

Briefly describe your typical self-talk style around those two beliefs

____

____

How are your subconsciously absorbed beliefs impacting your self-talk and what do you need to do about it?

____

What strategy is helping you identify and alter your self-talk successfully?

____

____

Diving deeper

You may not have realized it, but as you go about you daily routines you are continually thinking about and interpreting what you are seeing and hearing. And it's the internal voice inside your head that impacts how you perceive every situation. No doubt much of your self-talk is positive: 'I'd better get off the couch and mow the lawn' or 'I'm really looking forward to going on vacation with my family.' However, it is your negative self-talk that can become unrealistic or self-defeating: 'I'm never going to be able to walk a mile. Who am I kidding?' or 'Go a day without chocolate? You've got to be joking!'

Self-talk follows thoughts, and sometimes it's just plain erroneous. You can test, challenge, and change your self-talk. If you recognize erroneous self-talk, challenge the erroneous parts and replace them with more reasonable thoughts.

Sit down and close your eyes. Become mindfully aware of the self-talk that is flying around inside your head and listen to it carefully for three or four minutes.

How happy are you with the self-talk patterns you have identified? ________

____

If no, what is your strategy for handling your self-talk challenges? ________

____

____

Looking forward, what will you do differently about your self-talk? ________

____

____

Counting Conundrum

Reinforcing what you learn

Ken imagined in his mind's eye what a Longevity Lifestyle would look like for him. Picturing this gave his brain a map to follow.

Does your mindset include the following three items?

Yes	No	
❐	❐	1. A workable plan to create a brain-based Longevity Lifestyle?
❐	❐	2. An understanding of the benefits of optimum nutrition as well as appropriate exercise?
❐	❐	3. A commitment to create and maintain this style of living for the rest of your life?

Write how you are addressing any 'No' and turning it into a 'Yes:'

____

____

List ONE new key point you learned in Chapter 10.

____

____

Waste or Waist

Reinforcing what you learn

Individuals who embrace a Longevity Lifestyle tend to think in terms of decades rather than years. Human beings are the only creatures capable of taking a long view—but that requires goal-setting, mindful awareness, and personal committement. Keeping a record of what you eat and drink for three to seven days periodically is a proven strategy for helping you analyze what you really are ingesting and maintain an optimum weight.

❐ Yes ❐ No Have you kept a food journal for three to seven days?

If yes, what patterns did you identify about your eating habits? ____________

____

What surprised you most and least? ________________________________

____

What are you doing now to resolve inappropriate eating habits?

____

List ONE new key point you learned in Chapter 11.

____

____

Ultimate in Competition

Reinforcing what you learn

Roger learned that the hormones *ghrelin* and *leptin* function much as the gas and brake pedals do in a motor vehicle. You do have the ability to think ahead and put helpful strategies in place—if you choose to use it. Which of the following are you doing to keep ghrelin and leptin in balance?

- ❒ Avoiding eating or drinking 'empty calories'
- ❒ Avoiding over eating and implementing good portion control
- ❒ Avoiding poor quality foods in favor of high quality foods
- ❒ Eating only two or three bites of dessert if you choose to have dessert
- ❒ Eating slowly, chewing your food well, and enjoying what you eat
- ❒ Drinking a glass of water thirty minutes prior to your meal

A mindset of gobble 'till you wobble or glutton 'till you unbutton or binge 'till you cringe or scarf 'till you barf moves you away from—not toward—a balanced brain-based Longevity Lifestyle.
—Arlene R. Taylor

List ONE new key point you learned in Chapter 12.

____

____

Gifts for Yourself and Others

Overweight and obesity are not good for any brain—but they may be especially lethal for the female brain. Give yourself the gift of keeping your weight within your optimum range. Role-model and encourage your friends to do the same

The journal Neurology, reported that women who are obese throughout life are more likely to lose brain tissue and loss of brain tissue has been linked to cognitive decline. As the BMI of women in the research project increased, their risk of brain atrophy also increased thirteen to sixteen percent. Overweight or obesity also increased the risk of brain damage in the temporal lobe, involved with language, memory, and hearing.

Adult obese women showed increased risk of brain atrophy (shrinkage), which increases their risk for brain damage. A higher BMI was associated with shrinkage in every region of the cortex. A report in the Journal of the American Geriatric Society indicated that the higher a woman's weight and BMI, the worse off the woman was in terms of brain function.

Obesity is the terror within. Unless we do something about it, the magnitude of the dilemma will dwarf 9-11 or any other terrorist attempt.
—Richard Carmona

Thinking Ahead

Name two people who would appreciate the gift of you avoiding or minimizing brain shrinkage and brain damage.

1. ______________________________ 2.________________________________

Living Younger Longer

As you age you can gain perspective on gender relationships, understand more about gender differences, practically apply what you learn, communicate more effectively with the opposite gender—and even have more fun doing it

About forty percent of a man's body is muscle tissue, which burns five more calories per pound than fat tissue—even at rest, so males generally find it easier to lose weight. With a greater fat-to-muscle ratio, females find it more difficult to lose weight (prevention is easier than cure). Male muscles are less well equipped to deal with changes in hormonal levels and water retention, however. Males tend to experience more muscle aches and pains with a cold or flu. In addition, the preoptic nucleus—a part of the brain that registeres temperature—is larger in the male brain with more temperature receptors, so as their body temperature rises, males feel symptoms more intensely.

Think of male speech and female speech as differing spoken languages, as well, that underlie all other languages and dialects on the planet. Male speech is a language of independence, used to direct, instruct, exhibit skill, negotiate, convey information, negotiate, and preserve autonomy. Female speech is a language of connection, used to create intimacy, establish rapport, express feelings, nurture, and process information.

Circle the number that represents how gender-bilingual you are.

1-----2-----3-----4-----5 Scale: 1 = low and 2 = high

Use Your Neurons! Come on—you can do it!

Joan's mother had three children. The first was named April, the second May. What was the name of the third child?

My Notes

(Your name) ________, you are remembering this:

You must think of yourself as

becoming the person

you want to be.

—David Viscott

Welcome to Section 6

Record your measurements in the Appendix

Eating *fewer* healthier carbs may not be the ticket. Eating moderate amounts of healthier carbs likely is. They help supply your brain and body with the neurotransmitter serotonin, which impacts appetite, mood, and sleep, among other things. It's a cascade effect: eat healthier carbs, blood-sugar levels rise appropriately, and insulin is released to help the amino acid tryptophan move into the brain where it ultimately creates serotonin. Too few carbs and too little serotonin can contribute to fatigue, irritability—and may even lead to depression. Too few healthy carbs may be one of the reasons that habitual dieters may have low serotonin levels in both their brain and gastrointestinal tract—a situation that can lead to bingeing.

Read Chapters 13-14 and the Mediterranean Way

Checking-In

Setting SMART goals is one of your keys for success. SMART goals are *Specific*, *Measurable*, *Attainable*, *Realistic*, and *Timely*. "I'd like to eat healthier" is difficult to measure and nearly impossible to account for over time.

A goal that better meets SMART criteria would be, 'You are eating two servings of fruits and two servings of vegetables six days a week for the next two months. Then you will reevaluate your progress.' This goal is well defined and allows you to meet and measure your progress over time. The point is that you are not limited to simply reacting to events: You can take SMART steps to set SMART goals to help you achieve a SMART brain-based Longevity Lifestyle.

People with goals succeed because they know where they are going. It's as simple as that.
—Earl Nightingale

Write down your SMART goal for the next seven days.

____

Check if your goal meets the elements of a SMART goal.

		Yes	**No**
S	Specific	❐	❐
M	Measureable	❐	❐
A	Attainable	❐	❐
R	Realistic	❐	❐
T	Timely	❐	❐

It is a most mortifying reflection to consider what you have done compared to what you might have done.

—Samuel Johnson
In Boswell's
Life of Johnson 1770

Diving Deeper

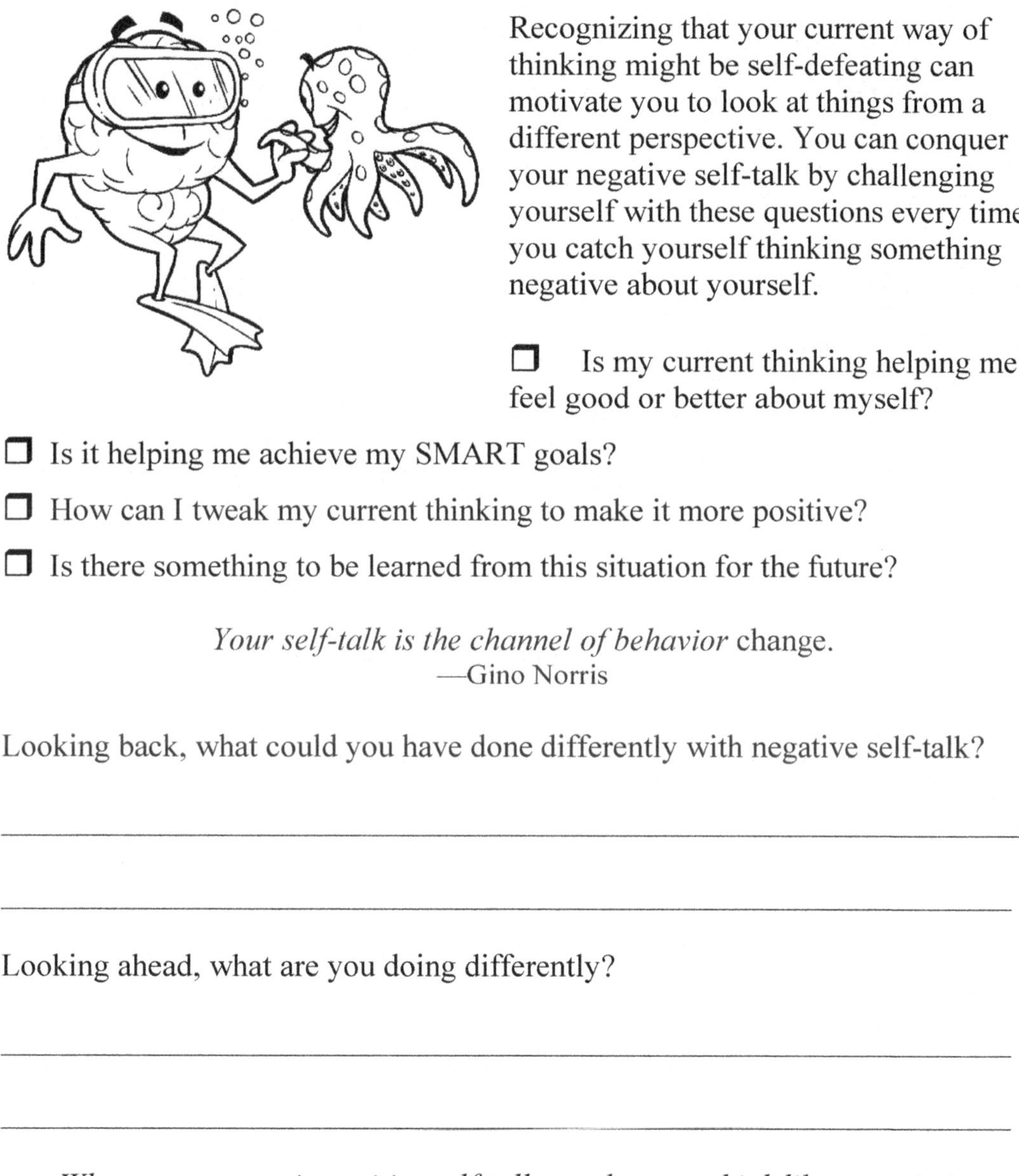

Recognizing that your current way of thinking might be self-defeating can motivate you to look at things from a different perspective. You can conquer your negative self-talk by challenging yourself with these questions every time you catch yourself thinking something negative about yourself.

❒ Is my current thinking helping me feel good or better about myself?

❒ Is it helping me achieve my SMART goals?

❒ How can I tweak my current thinking to make it more positive?

❒ Is there something to be learned from this situation for the future?

Your self-talk is the channel of behavior change.
—Gino Norris

Looking back, what could you have done differently with negative self-talk?

____

____

Looking ahead, what are you doing differently?

____

____

When you engage in positive self-talk, you learn to think like an optimist. As an optimist you will be able to visualize more options and solutions to your problems. Your problem solving abilities will improve. As an optimist you will be less prone to giving into defeat.
—Richard B. Rosse

Food Wise and Fat Smart

Reinforcing what you learn

Marjorie learned that dieting is not a desirable strategy in the long term. Circle the number of times you've gone on a diet of any type in an attempt to lose weight?

1---2---3---4---5---6---7---?_____

What's your history? Write it below.

Dieting ____

Weight Loss ____

Some still believe that eating a low-carb, high-fat diet is a better bet for weight loss. Dr. Brinkworth and colleagues, Adelaide, Australia, conducted a randomized clinical trial of individuals who followed either a very-low-carb, high-fat diet OR a high-carb, low-fat diet for one year. It included assessments of mood and well-being. Average weight loss over the year was the *same* in both groups. Mood measurements, however, revealed a lasting improvement in only those following the high-carb, low-fat diet.

Reminder: A brain-based Longevity Lifestyle does not include dieting. It incorporates components in balance. This includes quality nutrition along with portion control of healthier carbs and plant-based proteins and fats.

List ONE new key point you learned in Chapter 13.

____

____

GI, GL, and G-Willie Willikers

Reinforcing what you learn

Belle learned a Longevity Lifestyle can help reduce the risk of some chronic diseases. Below, check which types occur in your biological family system?

❒ Type 1 diabetes ❒ Type 2 diabetes
❒ Overweight ❒ Obesity

❒ Heart disease	❒ Allergies	❒ Osteoarthritis
❒ Cancer	❒ Asthma	❒ Auto-immune disease
❒ Glaucoma	❒ Dementia	❒ Rheumatoid arthritis
❒ Stroke	❒ Seizures	❒ ____________________

Have you ever been called a 'fat head?' That describes the brain! Axons, the long projections from some neurons, are wrapped in myelin. The tissues that form myelin are built from lipoproteins (a substance composed of fat and protein). It's difficult to get a precise percentage but some estimate myelin is about forty percent water, with the remaining sixty percent tissue composed of one fourth protein and three fourths fat. Much like fiber optics, the myelin sheath enables electrical impulses to travel along the axons quickly and smoothly—if damaged, transmission can be impaired. In adults, damage may occur from a stroke, inflammation, immune disorder, metabolic disorder, and nutritional deficiencies (e.g., lack of vitamin B12). Omega-3, an essential fatty acid, is important to myelin-sheath health.

List ONE new key point you learned in Chapter 14.

____

____

The Mediterranean Way

Reinforcing what you learn

Review the list below and check any that are part of your current brain-based Longevity Lifestyle:

❑ Choosing raw and dry-roasted nuts rather than those roasted with oils and salt

❑ Minimizing fried and deep-friend foods

❑ Including foods high in potassium for sodium-potassium balance

❑ Using herbs and spices for flavoring instead of salt only

❑ Substituting avocado for dairy cheese in tacos and cooking

❑ Replace sodas, regular and diet, juices, and sugary drinks with water

❑ Using cold-pressed olive oil for salads and coconut oil for cooking

❑ Minimizing the use of animal-based products and moving toward the use of plant-based products including healthier high-quality carbs

I am only one, but still I am one. I cannot do everything, but still I can do something; and because I cannot do everything, I will not refuse to do something that I can do.

—Helen Keller

List ONE new key point you learned from reading about the Mediterranean Way in the Appendix.

____

____

Gifts for Yourself and Others

Shrink your waistline—with the goal of reducing your risk of developing diabetes type 2, memory loss, and dementia

The average male would do well to keep his waistline at 40 inches (102 cm) or less; the average female at 35 inches (89 cm) or less

The results of a sixteen-year study reported in The New England Journal of Medicine indicated that overweight or obesity was the single most important predictor of type 2 diabetes and that the majority of cases of type 2 diabetes could be prevented by the adoption of a healthier lifestyle.

In a separate study, researchers at Rush University reported that individuals with excess fat around the middle are more than three times as likely to develop memory loss and dementia later in life compared with those who have a svelte waistline. Scientists believe that the liver has to work harder in people with excess belly fat. This uses up more of a protein called PPARalpha, which depletes levels in the brain. This is the same protein the hippocampus uses it to process memory and when it cannot get sufficient amounts, its functions can be impaired. Overweight and obesity happen one bite at a time, one ounce at a time, and one pound at a time. Fortunately, so do prevention and weight management.

Thinking Ahead

Who in your life would appreciate the gift of you reducing your risk for chronic illnesses?

1. __________________________ 2. __________________________

Living Younger Longer

You are living in the 'Age of the Brain' with its wealth of information from sciences that include PNI or Psychoneuroimmunology, Epigenetics, and Brain Function. Lucky you!

PNI has discovered that every thought you think alters your neurochemistry and affects every cell in your body. Avoid whining or complaining or blaming about what you are no longer able to do and focus instead on what you can do to live a healthy, productive, happy life. There has never been another brain like yours nor will there ever be. You can make a difference on this planet in a way that no other brain can contribute. Find a way to contribute. Role-model the joy of living a brain-based Longevity Lifestyle. You are growing older anyway, so you may as well do it gracefully and with style—yours!

It is in this whole process of meeting and solving problems that life has its meaning. Problems are the cutting edge that distinguishes between success and failure. Problems call forth our courage and our wisdom; indeed, they create our courage and wisdom. It is only because of problems that we grow mentally and spiritually.

—M. Scott Peck

Use Your Neurons! Come on—you can do it!

Daffynitions—they help you look at things in a new way.

Selfish	What the owner of a seafood store does
Relief	What trees do in the spring
Paradox	Two healthcare professionals
Heroes	What a man in a boat does
Avoidable	What a matador tries to do
Handkerchief	Cold storage
Raisin	A grape with a sunburn

My Notes

(Your name) ________, you

are remembering this:

s

____

Be the change you want to

see in the world.

—Mohandas Karamchand Gandhi
(Mahatma Gandhi)

Welcome to Section 7

Record your measurements in the Appendix

Studies suggest that eating healthier carbs—ancient grains such steel-cut oats, amaranth, basmati brown rice, rye and millet, along with seeds like chia, teff, sunflower, flax, hemp, and quinoa—may help keep you younger for longer. Rich sources of fiber, these types of healthier carbs not only fill you up and support a healthy gastrointestinal system but also contribute antioxidants to protect your cells from the effects of damaging chemicals, toxins, and free radicals, all of which contribute to chronic illness and disease. The goal, of course, is to slow down your rate of biological aging and retard the onset of symptoms of aging—in so far as it is possible to do so.

Read Chapters 15-17

Checking-In

What is helping you to stay motivated, engaged, enthusiastic, and rewarded to create and maintain a Longevity Lifestyle?

- ❒ Laughing more every day
- ❒ Developing better nutrition
- ❒ Thinking more clearly
- ❒ Increasing my energy levels
- ❒ Discarding negative thinking
- ❒ Exercising more and sensing the results
- ❒ Learning new information about the brain
- ❒ Doing good self-care consistently for the first time in my life
- ❒ Choosing to become more hopeful about the future
- ❒ Setting priorities and sticking to them
- ❒ Learning more about the process of growing older
- ❒ Developing a healthy sense of humor
- ❒ Implementing strategies for preventing chronic diseases
- ❒ Looking better and feeling better

List three factors that you are allowing to interfere with your success

1. ______________________________
2. ______________________________
3. ______________________________

What actions are you taking to stop interference from each of those factors?

1. ______________________________
2. ______________________________
3. ______________________________

Action expresses priorities.
—Mahatma Gandhi

Diving Deeper

Although centenarians often share some things in common, differences outweigh similarities. Studies found that people who live to be over one hundred have differing social and economic levels, education, work experience, religious beliefs, and level of prosperity. This is good news! Some factors seem to stand out, however. Which of the following are in your Longevity Lifestyle tool kit?

- ❒ Believing that your choices matters and that you can make a difference
- ❒ Possessing common sense to deal with everyday problems effectively
- ❒ Taking steps to voiding infectious diseases, falls, and head injuries
- ❒ Understanding that it is rarely too late to make positive changes
- ❒ Implementing effective stress-management strategies and skills
- ❒ Using positive self-talk consistently with yourself and others
- ❒ Learning from your mistakes *and* from your successes
- ❒ Packing a PAC mindset with you everywhere
- ❒ Laughing a lot and honing a sense of humor
- ❒ Enjoying surprises and new experiences
- ❒ Honing skills of Emotional Intelligence
- ❒ Choosing health-promoting behaviors
- ❒ Setting and achieving goals abd enjoying life satisfaction

We've all heard that you have to learn from your mistakes, but I think it's more important to learn from your successes. If you learn only from your mistakes, you are inclined to learn only errors.
—Norman Vincent Peale

What was your biggest success this week and what did you learn from it?

____

____

Ecstasy Excess

Reinforcing what you learn

Harry learned that studies have shown people often gravitate toward specific foods based on whether they feel happy or sad, content or anxious, angry or fearful. This is referred to as *emotional eating*. What comfort foods have you identified?

- ❒ Salty foods
- ❒ Sweet foods
- ❒ Cheesy foods
- ❒ Sour or savory foods
- ❒ Chewy foods
- ❒ Soft or smooth foods
- ❒ Hot foods
- ❒ Cold foods
- ❒ Other ______________________________

If you gravitated toward them during the last few days, identify the reason.

____

When you begin to feel irritated, refrain from speaking irritably and from eating impulsively. Count to ten. Say to yourself: 'Something triggered your irritation. There is some reason behind it. Dig to discover the reason.' Drink a glass of water and keep your mind busy figuring it out. Your brain knows. Direct it to share the information with you. Speaking words you *may* regret or eating calories you *will* regret is not a solution—just an overreaction.

List ONE new key point you learned in Chapter 15.

____

____

When Smaller Is Better

Reinforcing what you learn

Juliette and Jeanette, learned that portion size can impact person size. If you were raised before 1970, chances are your parent(s) probably played a major role in what you ate as a child. Most meals were eaten at home and foods and portions often were preselected for you. If you did not learn portion control during childhood, you'll need to learn it in adulthood.

Below, check all that apply related to how you currently manage portion control

- ❒ Never think about it
- ❒ Too much trouble
- ❒ Don't know how
- ❒ Try to be portion-reasonable
- ❒ Eat until I'm full and forget about it
- ❒ Overeat on what I like
- ❒ Binge and then feel guilty
- ❒ Other____________________

If what you're doing isn't working well, what are you doing differently?

____

____

List ONE new key point you learned in Chapter 16.

____

____

IQ Plus EQ Equals SQ

Reinforcing what you learn

John and Joan learned that family scripts are more powerful than they had previously realized, and that they can trigger negative or positive behaviors. As Denis Waitley put it: *You are your own scriptwriter and the play is never finished, no matter what your age or position in life.* There is always editing to do.

What 'script' behaviors tend to result in negative outcomes? ______________

____

____

What 'script' behaviors result in positive outcomes? ______________

____

____

To be authentic is literally to be your own author, to discover your own native energies and desires, and then to find your own way of acting on them.
—Warren G. Bennis

List ONE new key point you learned in Chapter 17.

____

____

Gifts for Yourself and Others

Your heart is working every nanosecond of your life—faithfully doing its part to keep you going on your Longevity Lifestyle. Thank your heart, and give it a break by reducing the number of miles of blood vessels through which it must pump your blood!

Depending on height and weight, estimates are that average body contains from 60,000 to 100,000 miles of blood vessels. Estimates range from 7 to 100 miles of new blood vessels required for each pound of excess fat. Take the low estimate or the high estimate—either way it's no wonder obesity and heart disease go hand in hand. Imagine your heart having to work harder and harder and harder to pump your blood through extra miles of blood vessels. Talk about 'going out of your way' on your life's journey!

The National Institute of Health (National Heart, Lung, and Blood Institute) points out that as your body mass index (BMI) rises, so does your risk for Coronary Heart Disease (CHD). Overweight and obesity puts you at a higher risk for high blood pressure, increased blood cholesterol and triglyceride levels, and heart disease (to say nothing of strokes).

When you reach an optimum weight range, what happens to all those blood vessels that no longer are needed to nourish those 'lost' pounds? The good news is that your body re-absorbs the now unnecessary blood vessels. Nothing is lost and much is gained.

Thinking Ahead

Who in your life would benefit by you reducing your risk for heart disease?

1. ______________________________ 2. ______________________________

Living Younger Longer

By living longer with good levels of mental, emotional, physical and spiritual function, you gain additional time to aim higher. Remember, more than half the factors that have been found to impact aging are within your partial if not complete control.

Nearly a decade ago, Dr. Walter M. Bortz II, Clinical Associate Professor at Stanford University and co-chair of the AMA-ANA Task Force on Aging estimated that the human body is programmed to last one or two decades past the century mark.

If you don't sabotage its natural process, your chances of making it to age 120 are excellent.
—Walter M. Bortz II MD

Because the mind influences every cell in the body, human aging is fluid and changeable; it can speed up, slow down, stop for a time and even reverse itself.
—Deepak Chopra MD

You control how healthy you are . . . and how long you are going to live . . . there is no biological reason why we cannot live to be over age 100.
—Dr. Robert Willix Jr.

Use Your Neurons! Come on—you can do it!

7H15 M3554G3 53RV35 7O PR0V3 H0W 0UR M1ND5 C4N D0 4M4Z1NG 7H1NG5! 1MPR3551V3 7H1NG5! 1N 7H3 B3G1NN1NG 17 WA5 H4RD BU7 N0W, 0N 7H15 LIN3, Y0UR M1ND 1S R34D1NG 17 4U70M471C4LLY W17H 0U7 3V3N 7H1NK1NG 4B0U7 17. B3 PROUD! 0NLY C3R741N P30PL3 C4N R3AD 7H15.

My Notes

(Your name) _______, you are remembering this:

Success is a process, a quality

of mind, and a way of being.

—Alex Noble

Welcome to Section 8

Record your measurements in the Appendix

Avoid refined and highly processed carbs, especially when combined with hydrogenated or partially hydrogenated fats, trans fats, and sugar. Instead, choose those that are unrefined—foods in as natural a state as possible. Watch out for 'carb myths' and course correct as needed. Researchers studied groups of individuals and analyzed their intake of carbohydrates. Those who consumed forty-five to sixty-four percent of their total calories from healthier carbs showed the lowest risk of being overweight or obese. They found that adults with higher intakes of healthier carbs actually weighed *less* than those with lower intakes.

Read Chapters 18-19 and the Appendix Shopping Reminder

Checking-In

You teach people how to treat you, what to expect from you, what you and what you will accept or tolerate from them. Only you can change that. Check any of the following that are true for you.

- ❒ Low self-worth so over-perform
- ❒ Insecure so try to be perfect
- ❒ Do for others so they'll like me
- ❒ Easier to do it than teach how
- ❒ Allow myself to be abused
- ❒ Work ethic from childhood
- ❒ Want everything to be flawless
- ❒ Want to look good to others
- ❒ Poor or inconsistent boundaries
- ❒ Do it for 'church' or 'God,' after all
- ❒ Trouble holding others accountable
- ❒ Other________________________

Check any of the following factors that you perceive are pulling you away from making a Longevity Lifestyle an absolute priority.

- ❒ Self (must put others first)
- ❒ Can't say 'no' to self or others
- ❒ Parents or in-laws
- ❒ Siblings / other family member
- ❒ Spouse / partner
- ❒ Children
- ❒ School
- ❒ Church or club
- ❒ Fatigue / loss of sleep
- ❒ Feel guilty or shamed
- ❒ Numb out with food / overeating
- ❒ Zone out with TV or video games
- ❒ Dehydration from lack of water
- ❒ Lack of physical exercise
- ❒ Trying to be perfect / do it all right
- ❒ Other___________________

What specific steps are you taking to alter these patterns?

____

____

Diving Deeper

Everything in the universe ages and there are no guarantees. Nevertheless, studies indicate there are things you can do to help healthier aging. Check any of the following you have in place:

- ❐ Building in back-up plans
- ❐ Estimating consequences
- ❐ Stress-management strategies
- ❐ Effective self-care plans
- ❐ Strategies for handling change
- ❐ Solid social network
- ❐ Other ____________________
- ❐ Other ________________________

Which core emotions surface when you slip up on your goal(s) or program?

❐ Fear ❐ Anger ❐ Joy ❐ Sadness

Which emotional interrupters or motivators tend to arise in your life with a core emotion? They usually represent learned reaction patterns so make sure you understand what they do and let go of unhealthy guilt and shame.

❐ Guilt ❐ Shame ❐ Surprise ❐ Disgust

Healthy guilt – an emotional interrupter to get your attention, it indicates that you made a mistake (e.g., violated a code of etiquette or conduct, were careless). It reminds you that you're human. All humans makes mistakes and you can learn a new way. It suggests you make restitution whenever and wherever possible. Unhealthy guilt is usually learned (often in childhood) and says that *you* are a mistake and nothing can remedy that.

Healthy shame – an emotional interrupter to get your attention, it triggers a sense of distress or dread from a recognition of your mistake. Unhealthy shame says you are a bad unworthy person and deserve humiliation—period—even without making any mistakes.

Surprise – an emotional motivator that can increase the strength of any core emotion, it indicates that you were not expecting what happened.

Disgust – an emotional motivator that can strengthen a core emotion with a sense of revulsion, a perception of extreme unpleasantness or offensiveness.

Room with a View

Reinforcing what you learn

Rick learned that every time he started to worry about his weight or become anxious about his eating habits his brain seemed to shutdown, a natural brain phenomenon known as *downshifting*.

When does your brain tend to downshift? _______

____

____

How often does your brain tend to get caught in the trap of worry and anxiety?

❒ Rarely ❒ Some ❒ Moderately ❒ Frequently

Worry is a thin stream of fear trickling through the mind. If encouraged, it cuts into a channel into which all other thoughts are drained.
—Arthur Somers

Typically you are not responsible for every thought that pops into your mind (unless you did something to put it there). All things being equal, however, you are responsible for the thoughts you hang onto and ponder. If you nurture fear, your brain will search for other past memories of fear and bring them to your awareness—which can make you more fearful. When the immediate (or imagined) danger is past, choose to think thoughts of gratitude.

List ONE new key point you learned in Chapter 18.

____

Sculpting and Resculpting

Reinforcing what you learn

Tami and Tad learned the importance of including foods that contain soluble and/or insoluble carbohydrate fiber in their daily menu choices.

Below, place a check beside the foods you have eaten recently that contained one or both of these important types of fiber.

Soluble Fiber

- ❒ Citrus fruit, plums, pears
- ❒ Carrots, peas, Chickpeas
- ❒ Beans, legumes (peanuts), nuts
- ❒ Apples and blueberries
- ❒ Cucumbers, asparagus, celery
- ❒ Strawberries, blueberries

Insoluble Fiber

- ❒ Seeds like flax, chia, quinoa
- ❒ Avocado, banana, guava
- ❒ Unsweetened coconut,
- ❒ Brown rice, rye, some grains
- ❒ Potatoes, zucchini, green beans
- ❒ Cruciferous vegetables

Both Soluble and Insoluble Fiber

❒ Oats ❒ Legumes ❒ Avocado

Many fruits and vegetables contain both types of fiber. They may be on one list or the other based on the percentage of each type of fiber. Internet resources sometimes list the percentage by each type of fiber.

List ONE new key point you learned in Chapter 19.

____

____

Shopping Reminders

Reinforcing what you learn

Shopping can be a challenge, especially when clever marketing entices you toward impulse purchases. To help combat that, make a list of what you intend to buy. If you are tempted by clever marketing, stop and count to ten. Ask yourself if that impulse purchase will move you toward or away from a Longevity Lifestyle. Then make your best choice.

List the top three food and beverage items that are most likely to tempt you for an impulse purchase.

1. ____________________ 2. ____________________ 3. ____________________

When do you usually shop? ❑ AM ❑ PM ❑ After work ❑ Evening

What is your best shopping time to avoid impulse purchases? _______________

Typically you are at higher risk for impulse buying if you shop without a list of items to purchase and when you are hungry.

List ONE new key point you learned while reviewing the Shopping Reminder in the Appendix.

____

____

Gifts for Yourself and Others

Of all components studied, exercise was the number one single contributor to longevity. Move it and use it or lose it!

Staying active can improve your speed of recall, release endorphins that help you be alert, decrease your risk for depression, enhance capillary growth around the brain neurons, increase neurotrophins that serve as food for neurons—and increase your potential longevity.

A study in Sweden found that people who were older than age seventy-five and who were physically active and joined in social activities lived an average of nearly five and a half years longer than their less active peers; while those age eighty-five or older had an extra four years of longevity. The most important single factor in the longevity of study participants was physical activity. In and of itself, physical activity was linked to an extra two or more years of life. Are you a good friend to your brain and your heart?

A friend is what the heart needs all the time.
—Henry Van Dyke

Getting older is unavoidable—falling apart is not.
—John J. Ratey

Thinking Ahead

Name two people who will benefit from you creating and maintaining a *Longevity Lifestyle*, retarding the onset of symptoms of aging, and living younger longer:

1. ______________________ 2. ______________________

Living Younger Longer

Growing older brings with it great freedom—it sets you free to be the person you've always wanted to be and to like that person.

You become kinder to yourself, less critical and more affirming and encouraging. You've become your own best friend and like yourself in a balanced, optimum way. You take responsibility for your choices and behaviors and their resulting consequences. You are learning (as the old saying goes) when to hold and when to pull the cord on your parachute. You minimize making excuses and have stopped 'blaming,' yourself or others. You regularly forgive yourself and others—for the health and longevity benefits that you receive.

Studies at the Energy and Protein Nutrition Laboratory of the United States Department of Agriculture found no differences in the efficiency with which different people metabolize food. The conclusion was that differences in weight typically result from excess eating or deficient exercise, or both. You are avoiding behaviors that tend to raise your fat set-point, including:

- A sedentary lifestyle with inadequate physical activity and exercise
- Overeating through unmanaged portion sizes and/or bolting down your food and ingesting hundreds of calories in a short amount of time
- Choosing low-quality and/or 'empty' calories

Use Your Neurons! Come on—you can do it!

Angelina was born on December 28th, yet her family always holds the annual celebration of her birth in summer time. How is that?

My Notes

(Your name) ________, you are remembering this:

Only one thing registers on the subconscious mind: repetitive application—practice!

—Grace Speare

Welcome to Section 9

Record your measurements in the Appendix

By now you are familiar with using the tools of Glycemic Index and Glycemic Load. Do you have a general internal mental picture of where your favorite carbs fall on the GI and the GL? Learn to use the GI and the GL as big-picture, ballpark guides. Rather than compulsively counting every calorie and thinking deprivation and loss, select foods with a low or moderate GI and GL and that align with your Longevity Lifestyle. Drink a glass of water fifteen to thirty minutes before eating. When you sit down at your meal, take small bites, chew well, and savor what you are eating. Put your utensils down between bites. Give your brain time to register what you are ingesting. It feels great to eat nutritious food, especially when you are physiologically hungry!

Checking-In

You received a *script* at birth that contained generational expectations and traditions, spoken and unspoken. You also absorbed attitudes, beliefs, and expectations—some of them subconsciously—related to food, overweight, and obesity. Customs in many cultures not only center on food and beverages but also relate to evidence of prosperity. For example, a man's ability to provide for his family may be shown by the 'size' of family members. Some families provided an excess of food, some not enough. Identifying your attitudes, beliefs, and expectations is part of a *forewarned-is-forearmed* strategy.

List one positive food-related expectation from childhood ________________

____

List one negative food-related expectation from childhood ________________

____

List two things you learned about eating habits _________________________

____

List your family's expectations related to overweight or obesity ___________

____

____

The greater danger for most of us is not that our aim is too high and we miss it, but that it is too low and we reach it.
—Michelangelo di Lodovico Buonarroti Simoni

Diving Deeper

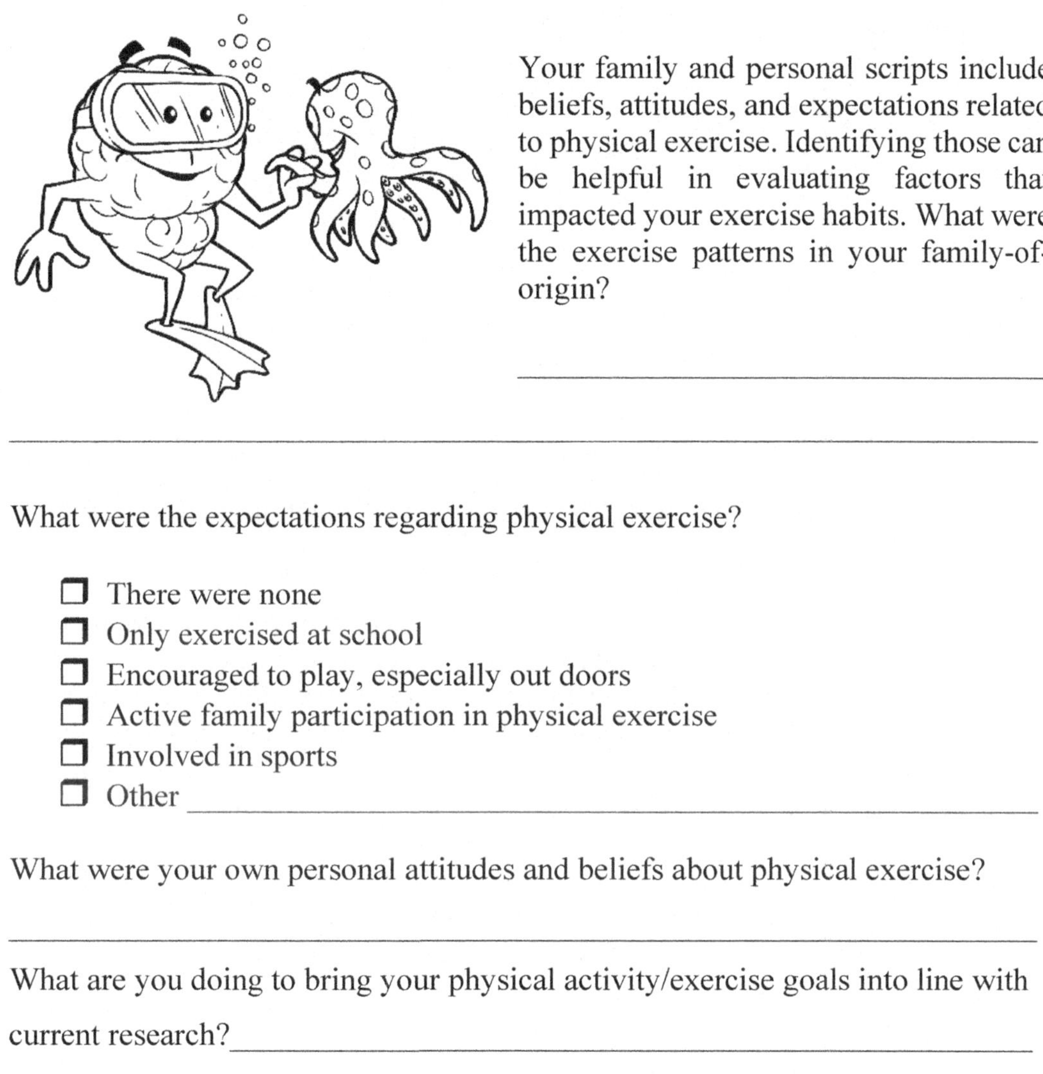

Your family and personal scripts include beliefs, attitudes, and expectations related to physical exercise. Identifying those can be helpful in evaluating factors that impacted your exercise habits. What were the exercise patterns in your family-of-origin?

____

____

What were the expectations regarding physical exercise?

- ❒ There were none
- ❒ Only exercised at school
- ❒ Encouraged to play, especially out doors
- ❒ Active family participation in physical exercise
- ❒ Involved in sports
- ❒ Other _______________________________

What were your own personal attitudes and beliefs about physical exercise?

____

What are you doing to bring your physical activity/exercise goals into line with current research?_______________________________

____

Think long term when making choices, even the ones that seem rather miniscule at the moment. Keep one eye on the impact those choices may have on your life down the line. For example, never start a relationship you know you'll want to end eventually. You never get your money's worth in those types of decisions—and they often cost you dearly.

—Anonymous

Three Pillars of Hedonia

Reinforcing what you learn

Xavier learned that breakfast boots up your brain much like you boot up a computer at the start of your work day.

List the healthier foods you eat for breakfast to boot-up your brain and jump-start your energy for the day.

Breakfast is such an important meal that skipping it may result in a forty percent loss of available energy by noon—and this may be the least of it. Researchers from the Harvard School of Public Health (HSPH) analyzed food-questionnaire data and health outcomes from 1992-2008 on 26,902 male health professionals ages 45-82. They found that males who regularly skipped breakfast had a 27 percent higher risk of heart attack or death from coronary heart disease than those who ate a morning meal. Non-breakfast-eaters were generally hungrier later in the day and ate more food at night, perhaps contributing to metabolic changes and heart disease. During the study 1,572 of the men had cardiac events.

Even after accounting for menu choices, physical activity, smoking, and other lifestyle factors, scientists found that the association between skipping breakfast and heart disease persisted. Missing that first meal of the day may increase your risk for factors including obesity, high blood pressure, high cholesterol, and diabetes, all of which may lead to a heart attack or other cardiac event over time.

List ONE new key point you learned in Chapter 20.

Case of the Gold Stars

Reinforcing what you learn

Marvin chose to stop drinking sodas and other sugary drinks and made pure water his beverage of choice.

What is your current beverage of choice? ______________________

Do you drink that throughout the day? ❒ Yes ❒ No

Below, circle Yes or No for each beverage depending on whether or not it aligns with a Longevity Lifestyle.

Beverage	Aligned?	Beverage	Aligned?
❒ Sodas	Yes No	❒ Tea	Yes No
❒ Juices	Yes No	❒ Beer	Yes No
❒ Water	Yes No	❒ Wine	Yes No
❒ Coffee	Yes No	❒ Spritzers	Yes No
❒ Water	Yes No	❒ Liquor	Yes No

Drinking water is like washing out your insides. The water will cleanse the system, fill you up, decrease your caloric load and improve the function of all your tissues.
—Kevin R. Stone

List ONE new key point you learned in Chapter 21.

____

____

Out of the Sand

Reinforcing what you learn

Metaphorically, Angela pulled her head out of the sand when she learned about the link between an optimum weight and healthier aging. Her coach told her: "You gained it—you can lose it. It's your choice."

Your current weight ________ Your optimum weight range ________________

List the two top contributors to what you weigh today:

1. ____________________________ 2. ________________________________

List two strategies you have implemented to reach your optimum weight range:

1. ____

2. ____

What is your main strategy for maintaining an optimum weight?

____

List ONE new key point you learned in Chapter 22.

____

____

Gifts for Yourself and Others

Your brain can only do what it thinks it can do. Help it understand not only what it can do but also what you want it to do

Your mindset, your thoughts, and your self-talk tell your brain not only what it can do but also what you want it to do. It's not always that you do not know what to do—rather it's often that you do not do what you know. You can enhance your likelihood of success. How you *do* what you *know* and *win*?

- Start and then keep on keeping on.
- Increase your knowledge so you know what to do.
- Tell your brain what it can do and what you want it to help you do.
- Practically apply what you know on a consistent basis.
- Use willpower to follow through on your healthier behaviors.
- Talk to yourself using your given name and the pronoun 'you'
- Use present tense as if what you want is already in place.

'Ellen, you are walking twenty minutes in the morning.'
'Ethan, you are in bed by ten o'clock every evening.'

Thinking Ahead

Name two people in your life who stand to benefit because you are role-modeling that you ***do*** what you ***know***:

1. ______________________________ 2. ______________________________

Living Younger Longer

You tend to avoid some stressors and manage those you can't avoid more effectively. You understand the 20:80 Rule and use it. You get more rest (itself a stress reducer)

Yale University researchers reported that high levels of cortisol (stress hormone) are associated with cravings for fatty snacks. Managing your stressors effectively is key in managing your health and weight. So is getting enough sleep. Sleep deprivation raises levels of ghrelin, a hormone that stimulates appetite and is associated with maintaining fat storage.

Columbia University Researchers reported that in comparison to study participants who slept 7-9 hours per night, participants who slept less than 4 hours nightly were 73 percent more likely to be obese; those who slept 6 hours nightly were 23 percent more likely to be obese; while those who slept an average of 10 hours a night were 11 percent less likely to be obese.

- ✓ Increase positive Eustress in your life; it helps you learn and grow.
- ✓ Avoid negative Distress whenever possible or reframe it.
- ✓ Identify hidden Misstress and minimize or manage it carefully; it can be as harmful over time as outright distress.
- ✓ Practice reframing. Turn Distress and Misstress into Eustress whenever possible.

Use Your Neurons! Come on—you can do it!

You are running a race and pass the person in second place. What position do you now hold?

My Notes

(Your name) ________, you are remembering this:

Concentrate all your thoughts upon the work at hand. The sun's rays do not burn until brought to a focus.

—Alexander Graham Bell

Welcome to Section 10

Record your measurements in the Appendix

Have you been trying to avoid all carbs? Think again! Not all carbs are created equal. Healthier carbs contribute to vitally important functions in the brain and body. They:

- Supply energy (glucose), especially for the brain, central nervous system, and muscles
- Prevent the breakdown of proteins (amino acids) as a source of energy
- Minimize ketosis from breakdown of fatty acids
- Assist with cellular and protein recognition
- Provide soluble and insoluble dietary fiber

Read Chapters 23-24

Checking-In

Cultures have socialized around food for so many eons that the two have become almost hand-in-glove. When planning nearly any event, food is typically near the top of the agenda. Identify your attitudes, beliefs, and expectations about food and socializing.

Instead of living the mantra 'food is fuel,' you may have been taught that 'food is social glue' or 'food is a love language' or 'you must eat whatever is offered to you or heaped upon your plate' or 'take seconds or thirds in order to please your mother or wife or hostess or chef or whomever.' Perhaps you were not permitted to leave the table until your plate was clean or you were shamed into overeating or under eating. Perhaps you were told: "Clean your plate. Remember there are starving children in other countries." Or, "Your mother slaved in the kitchen all day to provide this meal. Eat it." What were your childhood experiences?

1. What did you see role-modeled about food, expectations, and socializing?

____

____

2. What were you taught and what did you learn (they're not always the same)?

____

____

3. Are you clear about your own preferences? What are they?

____

____

Diving Deeper

Are you comfortable saying a simple, "No, thank you," when offered food/beverages you choose not to ingest? What strategies help you stay centered in a Longevity Lifestyle related to food and beverages at work or away from home?

____

____

____

Mark any of the following statements that apply to you

- ❒ I know what constitutes healthy food but can't take time to eat that way
- ❒ I have good boundaries when making food and beverage choices
- ❒ I usually buy what my family wants to eat even if I know better
- ❒ The 20:80 Rule is a big help when I am confronted with a stressor
- ❒ It is too much work to keep myself within an optimum weight range
- ❒ I rarely plan ahead for what to eat and just grab whatever is handy
- ❒ I tend to eat on the run because there is so much to do
- ❒ Being addicted to food is better than being addicted to tobacco or alcohol
- ❒ Schools are responsible for kids eating healthy and exercising regularly

Create a picture in your mind's eye of the behaviors you would exhibit around food and beverages if you believed you could live that way. List three key behaviors from your mental picture and then do something every single day to help you move those behaviors from imagination to reality.

1. ____

2. ____

3. ____

Crash and Burn or Not

Reinforcing what you learn

Mark learned that the brain is the first body system to recognize a stressor and it initiates the stress response within seconds (maybe nanoseconds). What key stressors have you identified?

❒ Safety issues ❒ Worry or anxiety ❒ Fear

❒ Relationships ❒ Family member ❒ Anger

❒ Expectations ❒ Finances ❒ Sadness

❒ Finances ❒ Work or career ❒ Illnesses

❒ Other ____

List two of your stressors for each of the following three categories

- Eustress ____
- Distress ____
- Misstress ____

List ONE new key point you learned in Chapter 23.

____

____

Forewarned Is Forearmed

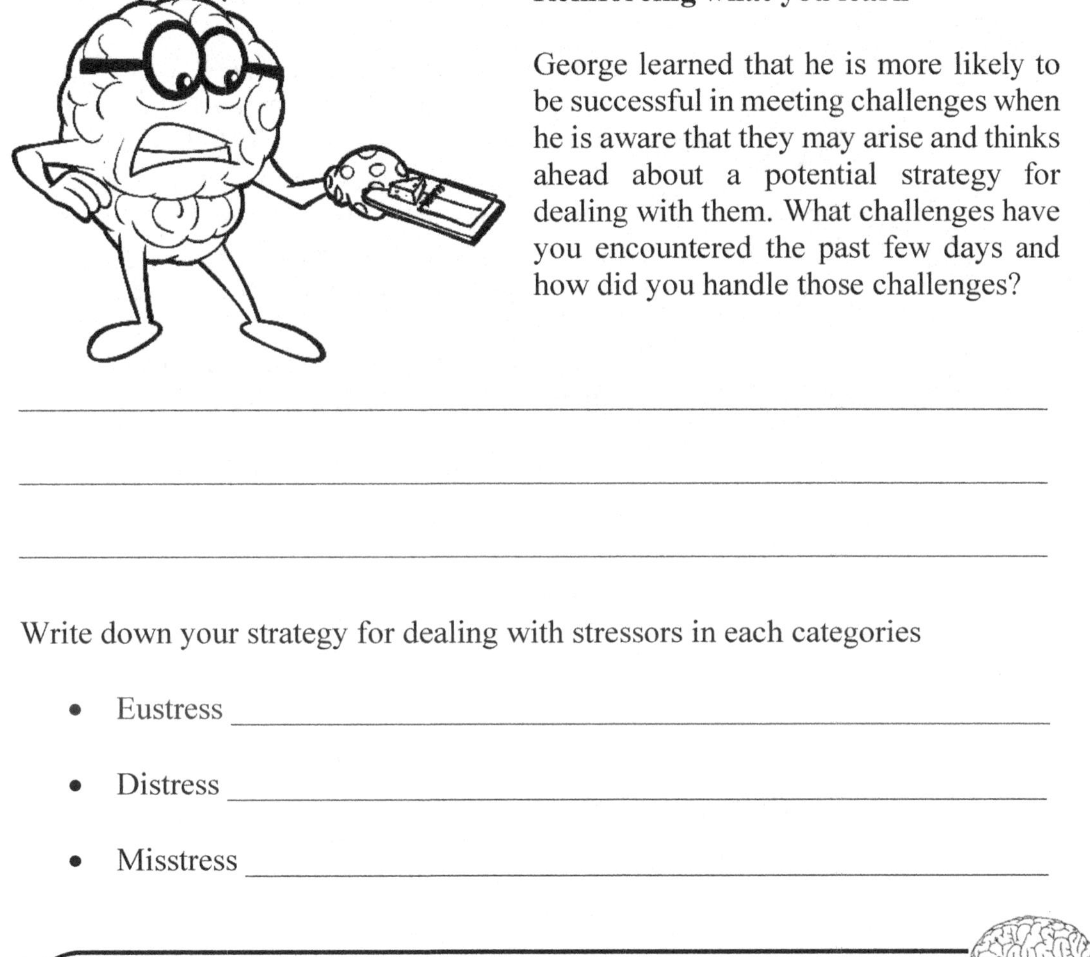

Reinforcing what you learn

George learned that he is more likely to be successful in meeting challenges when he is aware that they may arise and thinks ahead about a potential strategy for dealing with them. What challenges have you encountered the past few days and how did you handle those challenges?

____

____

____

Write down your strategy for dealing with stressors in each categories

- Eustress ____
- Distress ____
- Misstress ____

List ONE new key point you learned in Chapter 24.

____

____

Global Health Concerns

Reinforcing what you learn

There is international concern about the global pandemic of obesity it is linked with more than fifty diseases—including type 2 diabetes, heart disease, some forms of cancer, and dementia. The good news is that as you role-model a Longevity Lifestyle, you can influence those with whom you spend the most time, especially for smoking, happiness, health, and obesity.

List three important pieces of information you learned about global health concerns that you can practically apply in your life:

1. ______________________________

2. ______________________________

3. ______________________________

Obesity is associated with hyperactivation of the brain reward system for high-calorie (HC) versus low-calorie (LC) food cues, which encourages unhealthy food selection and overeating.
—Thilo Deckersbach PhD

List ONE new key point you learned about the Global Health Concerns section in the Appendix

____

____

Gifts for Yourself and Others

Raise your Emotional Intelligence Quotient or EQ. It is a gift that keeps on giving—to you and to your offspring generation after generation.

EQ is a label for a set of skills involving the ability to know what feels good, what feels bad, and how to get from bad to good in a way that results in positive outcomes. Raising your EQ offers many gifts that can help you to:

- Minimize conflict—and conflict is expensive, stressful, and even lethal
- Avoid JOT behaviors associated with low EQ such as jumping to conclusions, overreacting, and taking things personally
- Role model to others how to take responsibility for managing emotions and feelings appropriately
- Enhance your success. IQ plus EQ equals SQ or Success Quotient. Remember that EQ contributes an estimated 80 percent to your SQ, while IQ contributes only about 20 percent.

Depending where you begin, IQ may be raised from five to thirty points. The even better news is that EQ has no ceiling—the sky's the limit!

Thinking Ahead

Whose life potentially could be enhanced because you raised your level of Emotional Intelligence?

____

Living Younger Longer

You are able to make contributions to your own life as well as to that of family, friends, and community—that would likely not have happened otherwise

Many females do not figure out who they are innately until mid-life or later. Earlier they often were too busy caring for others. As their roles gradually change, they may be able to obtain the education or embark on the career they always wanted and often make their most significant contributions after menopause.

When they are young and just starting out, many males focus everything on building a career. It's on later on in life that they may realize the importance of relationships. They may devote more time to them, getting to know their grandchildren in a way they never knew their children, crafting a new connection with their wife or partner, and often making the contributions they are most proud of during retirement.

List one thing you've always wanted to do ______________________________

List one contribution you want to leave behind __________________________

Get going! What are you waiting for? Make it happen!

Use Your Neurons! Come on—you can do it!

A clerk in the butcher's shop, a dedicated competition runner, is 5 feet 11 inches tall, has long hair, and wears size 13 shoes. What does he weigh?

My Notes

(Your name) ________, you

are remembering this:

____

I look, feel, and behave several decades younger than my actual age, and much of that is because I believe you are what you think you are.

—Joan Collins

Welcome to Section 11

Record your measurements in the Appendix

Carbs are the preferred source of fuel for much of the work done by the brain and body. They provide energy for working muscles and fuel for the brain and central nervous system, without which weakness, dizziness, and low blood sugar (hypoglycemia) can occur. They also provide needed dietary fiber, both soluble and insoluble. Providing sufficient carbs in your daily cuisine can help prevent the body from trying to use proteins or fats for energy. The key? Eat at least half your calories in the form of healthier complex carbs—in as natural as state as possible.

Read Chapters 25-26

Checking-In

Check chapters with strategies that are helping you be successful; and check chapters with strategies that you still need to put in place.

Helped	Chapters	Need to put in place
❒	Where Rubber Meets the road	❒
❒	All about You	❒
❒	PAC for Success	❒
❒	Eavesdropping	❒
❒	White Bear	❒
❒	Besotted Brain	❒
❒	Slow and Steady	❒
❒	Death by Sitting	❒
❒	Booting up Your Brain	❒
❒	Counting Conundrum	❒
❒	Waste and Waist	❒
❒	Ultimate in Competition	❒
❒	Food Wise	❒
❒	GI, GL, and G-Willie-Willikers	❒
❒	Ecstasy Excess	❒
❒	When Smaller is Better	❒
❒	IQ plus EQ	❒
❒	Room with a View	❒
❒	Sculpting and Resculpting	❒
❒	Three Pillars	❒
❒	Case of Gold Stars	❒
❒	Out of the Sand	❒
❒	Crash and Burn	❒
❒	Forewarned is Forearmed	❒
❒	Elixir of Gratitude	❒

Diving Deeper

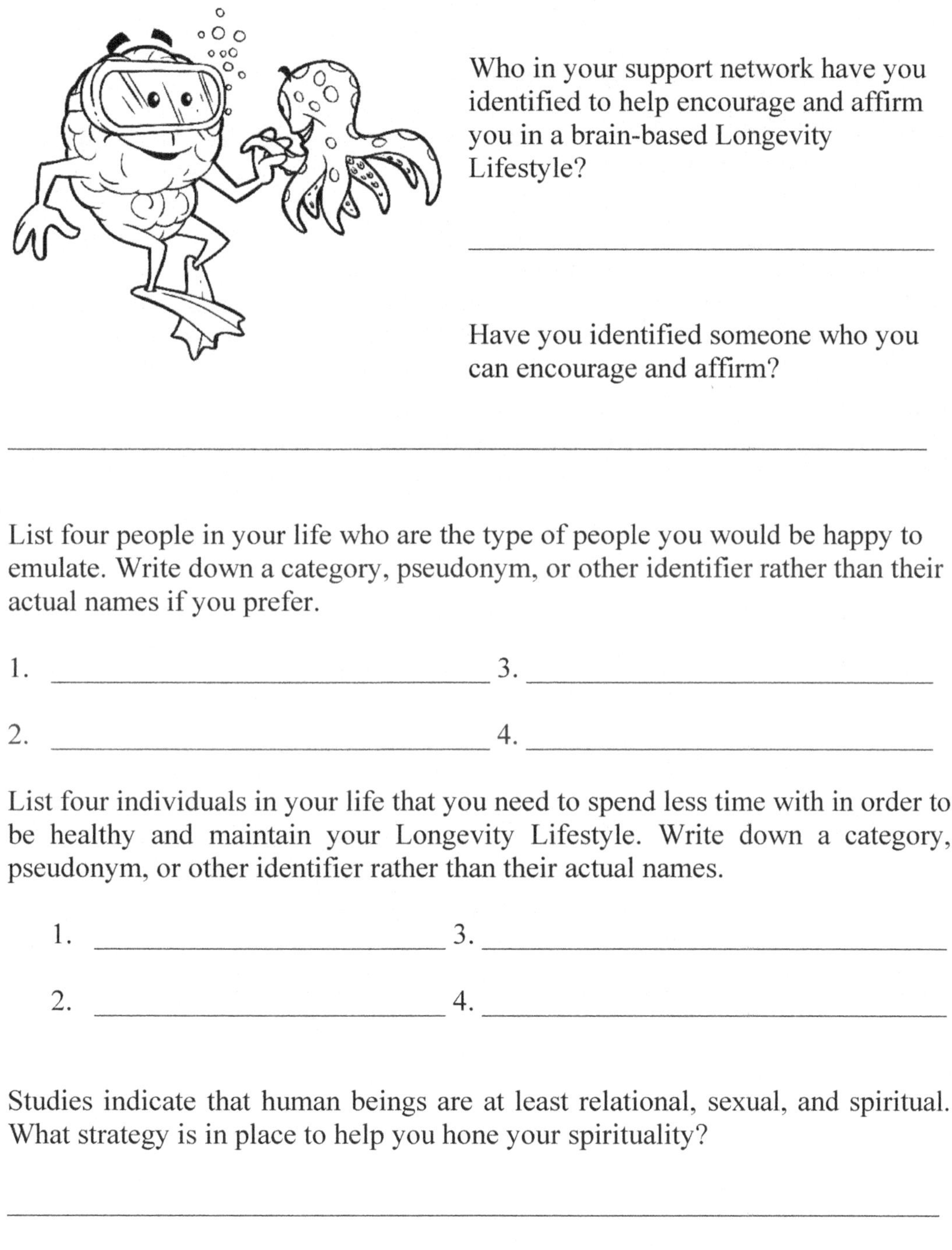

Who in your support network have you identified to help encourage and affirm you in a brain-based Longevity Lifestyle?

____

Have you identified someone who you can encourage and affirm?

____

List four people in your life who are the type of people you would be happy to emulate. Write down a category, pseudonym, or other identifier rather than their actual names if you prefer.

1. ______________________________ 3. ______________________________

2. ______________________________ 4. ______________________________

List four individuals in your life that you need to spend less time with in order to be healthy and maintain your Longevity Lifestyle. Write down a category, pseudonym, or other identifier rather than their actual names.

1. ________________________ 3. ______________________________

2. ________________________ 4. ______________________________

Studies indicate that human beings are at least relational, sexual, and spiritual. What strategy is in place to help you hone your spirituality?

____

____

Elixir of Gratitude

Reinforcing what you learn

Pax and Penny discovered they had slipped into the habit of noticing primarily the irritating things in life and had not realized the strong connection between spirituality, gratitude, forgiveness, and health. Think of your brain as a camera, continually recording whatever you place in working memory, the picture map for your brain to follow. What does your mental picture of yourself look like right now?

____

What does a mental picture of yourself twelve months from now look like?

____

What one thing are you doing to make this mental picture a reality?

____

The cards you're dealt do not matter so much as how you decide to play them. Decide to be successful. Decide to be happy. Truly decide to make a difference, and you will.
—Ralph Marston

List ONE new key point you learned in Chapter 25.

____

____

One, Two, Three—Go

Reinforcing what you learn

Debi, Dana, and Darla reported that embracing a Longevity Lifestyle was a factor in making it possible for them to make a longed-for visit to Peru.

What three things are you doing to keep your strategies front and center in your brain's working memory?

1. ______________________________

2. ______________________________

3. ______________________________

Question to Ponder

Are you living the 20:80 Rule? Are you becoming skilled at identifying the twenty percent of an event that you cannot do anything about (if you couldn't prevent it) and the eighty percent that is due primarily to what you think about the event and the weight you give to it? You can do almost everything about the eighty percent because your brain creates your perceptions.

List ONE new key point you learned in Chapter 26.

____

____

Gifts for Yourself and Others

According to Jean Marie Stine, affirmation is the mind's programming language. Hone this skill as a communication style for your own self-talk and when speaking to others.

Gratitude costs only a mindset, a choice, and an action—yours. Gratitude and spirituality are kissing cousins, to use an old expression. According to Alfred Painter, saying 'thank you' is far more than good manner; it is good spirituality. And spirituality involves the *spirit* with which you live life. Multiple studies have shown that gratitude, a form of affirmation, is a contributor to brain ad body health and potential longevity. Gratitude can even help you delay gratification, an important skill for success.

Unfortunately for some, as Eric Hoffer put it, the hardest arithmetic to master is that which enables you to count your blessings. Someone once described gratitude as the music of the heart when its chords are swept by the breeze of kindness. Help your heart sing today. Choose to be grateful.

> *An affirmation a day, keeps our negative thoughts away. An attitude of gratitude is life's most powerful affirmation! Affirmations are our mental vitamins—words with power. They provide the exquisite supplementary positive thoughts to enhance and balance the barrage of negative events and thoughts we experience daily. Affirmations affirm our soul and empower our mind in a most positive and tangible way.*
>
> —Angie Karan Krezos

Thinking Ahead

List two individuals with whom you shared the gift of gratitude today:

1. ______________________________ 2. ______________________________

Living Younger Longer

You have additional time to hone your sense of humor and learn to laugh at the vagaries of life. Learn to laugh at yourself and you'll have an endless supply of laughter triggers.

Studies have shown that very happy people (who tend to be healthy and long lived) laugh between a hundred and four hundred times a day. What is your daily average?

When someone says "You're over the hill," do you laugh because you know that being over the hill is better than being under the hill? When you hear, "I might as well be dead," do you think, 'Every day above ground is a good day?' When an individual says, "You're such a fat head!" do you chuckle because you know that the human brain actually does contain quite a bit of fat? Besides, that's just their brain's opinion and it may have little or nothing to do with your brain.

Redefine some common phrases and laugh: "Getting a little action" now means you don't need to take any extra fiber. "Getting lucky" means you found your car in the parking lot—quickly. Pulling an "all-nighter" means not getting up to the toilet even once. Although you are serious about life, you've learned not to take every little thing too seriously, yourself included. It's such a relief and your family and friends love your company. Lee S. Berk PhD of Loma Linda University has pointed out that just the anticipation of a mirthful laughter experience boosts endorphins twenty-seven percent and human grown hormone eighty-seven percent. Most everything seems to go better with laughter. So laugh—and last!

Use Your Neurons! Come on—you can do it!

If a farmer has five haystacks in one field and four haystacks in the other field, how many haystacks would he have if he combined them all together in a different field?

Your Attitude (Mindset)

Charles Rozell 'Chuck' Swindoll, founder of *Insight for Living* that is headquartered in Plano, Texas, takes the 20:80 Rule a step farther. He wrote:

The longer I live, the more I realize the impact of attitude on life. Attitude, to me, is more important that facts. It is more important than the past, than education, than money, than circumstances, than failures, than successes, than what people may think, say, or do. It is more important that appearance, giftedness, or skill. It will make or break a company, a church, a home. The remarkable thing is we have a choice every day regarding the attitude we will embrace for that day. We cannot change our past. We cannot change the fact that other people will act in a certain way. We cannot change the inevitable. The only thing we can do is play on the one string we have and that is our attitude. I am convinced that life is ten percent what happens to me and ninety percent how I react to it. And so it is with you. We are in charge of our attitude.

Growing up, what was the prevailing attitude in your home?

___

During your childhood did you copy the attitude in your home?

___

Are you still hanging onto the same attitude from childhood?

___

If your attitude is positive, great. If not, what are you doing about it?

___

Make the 20:80 Rule part of your brain-based Longevity Lifestyle.

My Notes

(Your name) ________, you are remembering this:

____

____

____

____

____

____

____

____

____

____

Like overweight and obesity … most of the metabolic abnormalities also associated with poorer cognitive performance can be combated with healthy eating and lifestyle.

—Tufts University
Friedman School of Nutrition
Health & Nutrition Letter Vol 13G

Welcome to Section 12

Record your measurements in the Appendix

Some weight-loss diets advocate severely restricting all carbohydrates, claiming this is more effective in preventing cardiovascular disease as compared with balanced weight-loss strategies. Naude and colleagues compared the effects of low-carb versus balanced weight-loss programs in overweight and obese adults. In the minimum follow-up period of three months, the low carb approach showed no weight-loss advantage. Be carb smart. Avoid either extreme as outlined below.

Getting too many carbohydrates can lead to an increase in total calories, causing obesity. Not getting enough carbohydrates can cause a lack of calories (malnutrition) or an excessive intake of fats to make up the calories.
—Dietary Guidelines for Americans, 7th Edition

Review Authors and Resources in the Appendix

Checking-In

While you may have come to the last section of this *LLM Companion Notebook,* you are well on the road to creating and maintaining a Longevity Lifestyle. Write down the three most helpful strategies you now have in place to ensure your long-term success.

1. ____

2. ____

3. ____

Make music part of your life

Music has been found to have healing properties. It can improve sleep, reduce stress and anxiety, and provide a variety of supportive benefits for the brain and immune system. Studies have shown that listening to certain selections of Mozart's music can facilitate complex neuronal patterns that are involved in higher brain activities such as mathematics.

Remember, your brain is your most important musical instrument. If you once took music lessons, start practicing or playing or singing again. If you didn't, consider doing so now. Listen to music. Sing or hum whenever you can. Quality music is a 'healthy pleasure.' Music can activate and stimulate the temporal lobes of the brain, slow heart rate or speed it up, calm the brain, and provide comfort.

What one thing taught you the most during this LLM Program? ____________

____

Diving Deeper

What did you learn about yourself that surprised you? ____________________

____

What research topic did you find most frightening?

____

What research topic did you find most helpful? ____________________

____

What are you doing to engage in 'healthy pleasures' and have fun?

____

____

What are you doing about forgiveness? ____________________

> *When I was first ordained, I believed that over fifty percent of all problems were at least in part due to unforgiveness. After ten years in ministry, I revised my estimate and maintained that seventy-five to eighty percent of all health, marital, family, and financial problems came from unforgiveness. Now, after more than twenty years in ministry, I have concluded that over ninety percent of all problems are rooted in unforgiveness.*
>
> —Father Al Lauer

Are you forgiving yourself as well as others? Can you really afford to be unforgiving? Remember, unforgiveness is like taking poison and expecting it to kill the other person. The person who is unforgiving pays the highest price. Conversely, the person who forgive benefits the most. Get serious about forgiveness.

Program in Review

The further backward you look, the further forward you can see.

—Sir Winston Churchill

Which of the following are ***currently*** part of your lifestyle?

- ❒ PAC mindset
- ❒ Optimum sleep on a daily basis
- ❒ Appropriate hydration with water
- ❒ Brain protection strategies
- ❒ Physical activity and exercise
- ❒ Challenging brain stimulation
- ❒ Exposure to natural light
- ❒ Healthy nutrition eating style
- ❒ Pesco-vegetarian eating style
- ❒ Vegetarian or vegan style of eating
- ❒ Laughter and play
- ❒ Support network
- ❒ Positive self-talk style
- ❒ Balanced work-home life
- ❒ Stress Management
- ❒ High Emotional Intelligence
- ❒ Life satisfaction
- ❒ Fast, fatty, fried, frozen foods
- ❒ Sodas, sugary drinks, juices
- ❒ Regular meals/portion control
- ❒ Frequent snacking
- ❒ Desserts on a regular basis
- ❒ Beer, Wine, or Spritzers
- ❒ Tobacco in any form
- ❒ Mind-altering drugs
- ❒ Other ____________________

In the 1st Section you were asked to complete this same list. Turn to that section and compare your responses back then with those of today.

1st Section: _________ / 26 12th Section: _________ / 26

Gifts for Yourself and Others

Be very clear: your greatest wealth is the health and functionality of your brain and body—and they are irreplaceable. Give yourself and others those gifts!

According to Virgil, 'The greatest wealth is health.' Many others have weighed in with similar perceptions. Mahatma Gandhi pointed out: 'Health is the real wealth and not pieces of gold and silver.' Buddha taught, 'Health is the greatest gift.' Lao Tzu said, 'Health is the greatest possession.' An old Spanish proverb says, 'A man too busy to take care of his health is like a mechanic too busy to take care of his tools.' Richard Baker advocated, 'Never risk your health to get wealth because your health is the wealth of wealth.' The Dalai Lama was once asked what surprises him most. He reportedly replied: *'Man,' because he sacrifices his health in order to make money. Then he sacrifices money to recuperate his health. Then he is so anxious about the future that he does not enjoy the present. The result being that he does not live in the present or the future. He lives as if he is never going to die, and then he dies having never really lived.*

The good health of your brain and body is your greatest wealth. Picture how your 'health' and 'wealth' have increased during the past twelve weeks, and how both can continue to increase over time. Give yourself and role-model for others the ongoing gift of a Longevity Lifestyle—it matters. Invest wisely, use your resources wisely, share wisely, and enjoy life for a long time.

Thinking Ahead

List two individuals who have encouraged you in your decision to create and maintain a Longevity Lifestyle. Thank them for their support.

1. ______________________________ 2. ______________________________

Living Younger Longer

With more years under your belt and more water under (or over) the bridge, you may be able to recognize the big picture more quickly and identify what really truly matters

Concentrate your time, energy, money, and emphasis on what studies have shown can make a difference to your brain and immune system. The California Longevity Study reported that four simple direct threats are reliably known to be consistently bad for health and longevity and recommends that you do your best to avoid them: Toxins and Poisons, Exposure to Excessive Radiation, Infections, and Trauma (especially to the head). Studies by University of Chicago's Bernice Neugarten showed that the most important factor in healthy aging is *life satisfaction.* Older adults who have the attitude that life circumstances are manageable, meaningful, and that you are in control of your life (at least to some degree) tended to have stronger immune systems and better health. Your own lifestyle choices can matter more than your genetics. Remember, seventy percent of how long and how well you live is in your hands!

Use Your Neurons! Come on—you can do it!

Paraprosdokians can stimulate humor and creative thinking.

- The only constant in life is change
- Where there's a will—I want to be in it
- You're never too old to learn something stupid
- Change is inevitable, except from a vending machine
- War does not determine who is right—only who is left
- I never said it was your fault; I just said I was blaming you
- You don't need a parachute to skydive—only if you want to skydive again
- I was told to respect my elders but at my age it's getting harder to find any
- Knowledge is knowing tomatoes are fruits; wisdom is leaving them out of fruit salads

Happy Graduation!

You did it! You realized that you do impact the health and potential longevity of your brain and body. You stepped up to the plate and got started. You have twelve weeks of your Longevity Lifestyle journey under your belt and documented in your own personal play-book. As with many life journeys, you only *know* when you *go*—now you *know* that you are looking better and feeling better and thinking more clearly as you *go*.

Brain aging is optional if you diligently use the right strategies. Your day-to-day behavior is either accelerating this process or it is decelerating it…the one with more (brain) reserve tends to remain functional longer. Getting well is not just about becoming symptom-free, it's also about boosting brain reserve. This requires three simple strategies:

- *Possessing brain envy—you have to really care about it*
- *Avoiding anything that hurts your brain*
- *Engaging in regular brain-healthy habits*

Every day you are either boosting or stealing your brain's reserves; you are either aging or rejuvenating your brain. When you truly understand this concept, you have a lot more influence in how fast your brain ages. You can change your brain and change your life.'

—Daniel G. Amen MD
Change Your Brain Change Your Life

Reinforce what you are learning and stay enthusiastic by going through the *LLM textbook, Companion Notebook,* and audiobook on a regular basis. Each time you review the material and listen to the audiobook your brain will perceive something in a new way. Studies indicate that the average adult really 'learns' information and transfers it into long-term memory after going through it at least three or four times with mindful awareness. Study! Turn what you learn into personal knowledge. Practically apply it on a daily basis. Role-model a brain-based Longevity Lifestyle for as long as you live. May it be long and healthy and rewarding and productive and happy and life-satisfying!

Annual Celebration

Plan an annual celebration around this date to affirm and reward you and your brain for maintaining a Longevity Lifestyle. It need not be expensive; it does need to be fun! Plan it! Write the date on your calendar. Invite your friends. Do it! Love it! Celebrate your health and longevity. Role-model and inspire others.

Date and time ______________________________

Location ___________________________________

Menu ____

Plan something to trigger mirthful laughter. For instance, ask guests to write a humorous 'newspaper headline.' Here are examples to get them started.

- Miracle cure kills fifth patient
- Starvation can lead to health issues
- Homeless survive winter; now what?
- Meat head resigns
- Meeting on open meetings is closed
- Homicide victims rarely talk to police
- City unsure why the sewer smells
- Hospitals resort to hiring doctors
- Driver with 8 DUIs blames drinking problem
- Total lunar eclipse will be broadcast live on Northwest public radio
- Parents keep kids home to protest school closure
- Puerto Rican teen named mistress of the universe
- Barbershop singers bring joy to school for deaf
- Caskets found as workers demolish mausoleum
- Man accused of killing lawyer receives a new attorney
- Worker suffers leg pain after crane drops 800-pound ball on his head
- Seventeen remain dead in morgue shooting spree
- Statistics show teen pregnancy drops off significantly after age 25

My Notes

(Your name) ________, you are remembering this:

____

____

____

____

____

____

____

____

____

____

____

____

Success is a journey—

not a destination.

—Ben Sweetland

Weekly Comparison Form - Master

You may want to make additional copies to use as you go through the Companion Notebook again and again.

Record your measurements each week in the appropriate spaces

	Wk 1	Wk 2	Wk 3	Wk 4	Wk 5	Wk 6	Wk 7	Wk 8	Wk 9	Wk 10	Wk 11	Wk 12
BMI												
Weight												
Waist size												

Weekly Comparison Form

Record your measurements each week in the appropriate spaces

	1	2	3	4	5	6	7	8	9	10	11	12
BMI 26	25	25	25	26								
Weight 172	166	164	166	170								
Waist size 38	38	37	38	38								

Weekly Comparison Form

Record your measurements each week in the appropriate spaces

	1	2	3	4	5	6	7	8	9	10	11	12
BMI												
Weight												
Waist size												

Weekly Comparison Form

Record your measurements each week in the appropriate spaces

	1	2	3	4	5	6	7	8	9	10	11	12
BMI												
Weight												
Waist size												

Daily Goals Form – Master

You may want to make additional copies to use as you go through the Companion Notebook again and again.

Part ____	Sun	Mon	Tue	Wed	Thr	Fri	Sat
Water Goal Void a very pale / clear urine once a day							
Exercise Goal Do at least 15 minutes of physical exercise							
Breakfast Goal Eat breakfast, including a healthy carb							
Nutrition Goal Eat 1 serving of fruit and 2 of vegetables							
Sleep Goal Sleep between 6 and 8 hours in 24 hours							
Replacement Goal Substitute 1 healthier choice or behavior							
Add Your Own Goal							

Give yourself one point each day for each goal you met (including the goal you added). Points for the Week: ____

Daily Goals Form

1st Section	Sun	Mon	Tue	Wed	Thr	Fri	Sat
Water Goal Void a very pale / clear urine once a day							
Exercise Goal Do at least 15 minutes of physical exercise							
Breakfast Goal Eat breakfast, including a healthy carb							
Nutrition Goal Eat 1 serving of fruit and 2 of vegetables							
Sleep Goal Sleep between 6 and 8 hours in 24 hours							
Replacement Goal Substitute 1 healthier choice or behavior							
Add Your Own Goal							

Give yourself one point each day for each goal you met (including the goal you added). Points for the Week: ______

Daily Goals Form

2nd Section	Sun	Mon	Tue	Wed	Thr	Fri	Sat
Water Goal Void a very pale / clear urine once a day							
Exercise Goal Do at least 15 minutes of physical exercise							
Breakfast Goal Eat breakfast, including a healthy carb							
Nutrition Goal Eat 1 serving of fruit and 2 of vegetables							
Sleep Goal Sleep between 6 and 8 hours in 24 hours							
Replacement Goal Substitute 1 healthier choice or behavior							
Add Your Own Goal							

Give yourself one point each day for each goal you met (including the goal you added). Points for the Week: ________

Daily Goals Form

3rd Section	Sun	Mon	Tue	Wed	Thr	Fri	Sat
Water Goal Void a very pale / clear urine once a day							
Exercise Goal Do at least 15 minutes of physical exercise							
Breakfast Goal Eat breakfast, including a healthy carb							
Nutrition Goal Eat 1 serving of fruit and 2 of vegetables							
Sleep Goal Sleep between 6 and 8 hours in 24 hours							
Replacement Goal Substitute 1 healthier choice or behavior							
Add Your Own Goal							

Give yourself one point each day for each goal you met (including the goal you added). Points for the Week: __________

Daily Goals Form

4th Section	Sun	Mon	Tue	Wed	Thr	Fri	Sat
Water Goal Void a very pale / clear urine once a day							
Exercise Goal Do at least 15 minutes of physical exercise							
Breakfast Goal Eat breakfast, including a healthy carb							
Nutrition Goal Eat 1 serving of fruit and 2 of vegetables							
Sleep Goal Sleep between 6 and 8 hours in 24 hours							
Replacement Goal Substitute 1 healthier choice or behavior							
Add Your Own Goal							

Give yourself one point each day for each goal you met (including the goal you added). Points for the Week: ______

Daily Goals Form

5th Section	Sun	Mon	Tue	Wed	Thr	Fri	Sat
Water Goal Void a very pale / clear urine once a day							
Exercise Goal Do at least 15 minutes of physical exercise							
Breakfast Goal Eat breakfast, including a healthy carb							
Nutrition Goal Eat 1 serving of fruit and 2 of vegetables							
Sleep Goal Sleep between 6 and 8 hours in 24 hours							
Replacement Goal Substitute 1 healthier choice or behavior							
Add Your Own Goal							

Give yourself one point each day for each goal you met (including the goal you added). Points for the Week: ______

Daily Goals Form

6th Section	Sun	Mon	Tue	Wed	Thr	Fri	Sat
Water Goal Void a very pale / clear urine once a day							
Exercise Goal Do at least 15 minutes of physical exercise							
Breakfast Goal Eat breakfast, including a healthy carb							
Nutrition Goal Eat 1 serving of fruit and 2 of vegetables							
Sleep Goal Sleep between 6 and 8 hours in 24 hours							
Replacement Goal Substitute 1 healthier choice or behavior							
Add Your Own Goal							

Give yourself one point each day for each goal you met (including the goal you added). Points for the Week: __________

Daily Goals Form

7th Section	Sun	Mon	Tue	Wed	Thr	Fri	Sat
Water Goal Void a very pale / clear urine once a day							
Exercise Goal Do at least 15 minutes of physical exercise							
Breakfast Goal Eat breakfast, including a healthy carb							
Nutrition Goal Eat 1 serving of fruit and 2 of vegetables							
Sleep Goal Sleep between 6 and 8 hours in 24 hours							
Replacement Goal Substitute 1 healthier choice or behavior							
Add Your Own Goal							

Give yourself one point each day for each goal you met (including the goal you added). Points for the Week: __________

Daily Goals Form

8th Section	Sun	Mon	Tue	Wed	Thr	Fri	Sat
Water Goal Void a very pale / clear urine once a day							
Exercise Goal Do at least 15 minutes of physical exercise							
Breakfast Goal Eat breakfast, including a healthy carb							
Nutrition Goal Eat 1 serving of fruit and 2 of vegetables							
Sleep Goal Sleep between 6 and 8 hours in 24 hours							
Replacement Goal Substitute 1 healthier choice or behavior							
Add Your Own Goal							

Give yourself one point each day for each goal you met (including the goal you added). Points for the Week: ___________

Daily Goals Form

9th Section	Sun	Mon	Tue	Wed	Thr	Fri	Sat
Water Goal Void a very pale / clear urine once a day							
Exercise Goal Do at least 15 minutes of physical exercise							
Breakfast Goal Eat breakfast, including a healthy carb							
Nutrition Goal Eat 1 serving of fruit and 2 of vegetables							
Sleep Goal Sleep between 6 and 8 hours in 24 hours							
Replacement Goal Substitute 1 healthier choice or behavior							
Add Your Own Goal							

Give yourself one point each day for each goal you met (including the goal you added). Points for the Week: ________

Daily Goals Form

10th Section	Sun	Mon	Tue	Wed	Thr	Fri	Sat
Water Goal Void a very pale / clear urine once a day							
Exercise Goal Do at least 15 minutes of physical exercise							
Breakfast Goal Eat breakfast, including a healthy carb							
Nutrition Goal Eat 1 serving of fruit and 2 of vegetables							
Sleep Goal Sleep between 6 and 8 hours in 24 hours							
Replacement Goal Substitute 1 healthier choice or behavior							
Add Your Own Goal							

Give yourself one point each day for each goal you met (including the goal you added). Points for the Week: ___________

Daily Goals Form

11th Section	Sun	Mon	Tue	Wed	Thr	Fri	Sat
Water Goal Void a very pale / clear urine once a day							
Exercise Goal Do at least 15 minutes of physical exercise							
Breakfast Goal Eat breakfast, including a healthy carb							
Nutrition Goal Eat 1 serving of fruit and 2 of vegetables							
Sleep Goal Sleep between 6 and 8 hours in 24 hours							
Replacement Goal Substitute 1 healthier choice or behavior							
Add Your Own Goal							

Give yourself one point each day for each goal you met (including the goal you added). Points for the Week: ___________

Daily Goals Form

12th Section	Sun	Mon	Tue	Wed	Thr	Fri	Sat
Water Goal Void a very pale / clear urine once a day							
Exercise Goal Do at least 15 minutes of physical exercise							
Breakfast Goal Eat breakfast, including a healthy carb							
Nutrition Goal Eat 1 serving of fruit and 2 of vegetables							
Sleep Goal Sleep between 6 and 8 hours in 24 hours							
Replacement Goal Substitute 1 healthier choice or behavior							
Add Your Own Goal							

Give yourself one point each day for each goal you met (including the goal you added). Points for the Week: ___________

Track Your Intake - Master

You may want to make additional copies to use as you go through the Companion Notebook again and again.

Day _________ Record item, time, and amount for everything you eat and drink for 3-7 days. Do you see a pattern?

Breakfast	
Lunch	
Dinner	
Snacks	
Water (oz)	
Beverages	
Other	

Track Your Intake

Day __________Record item, time, and amount for everything you eat and drink for 3-7 days. Do you see a pattern?

Breakfast	
Lunch	
Dinner	
Snacks	
Water (oz)	
Beverages	
Other	

Track Your Intake

Day __________Record item, time, and amount for everything you eat and drink for 3-7 days. Do you see a pattern?

Breakfast	
Lunch	
Dinner	
Snacks	
Water (oz)	
Beverages	
Other	

Track Your Intake

Day __________ Record item, time, and amount for everything you eat and drink for 3-7 days. Do you see a pattern?

Breakfast	
Lunch	
Dinner	
Snacks	
Water (oz)	
Beverages	
Other	

Track Your Intake

Day __________Record item, time, and amount for everything you eat and drink for 3-7 days. Do you see a pattern?

Breakfast	
Lunch	
Dinner	
Snacks	
Water (oz)	
Beverages	
Other	

Track Your Intake

Day __________Record item, time, and amount for everything you eat and drink for 3-7 days. Do you see a pattern?

Breakfast	
Lunch	
Dinner	
Snacks	
Water (oz)	
Beverages	
Other	

Track Your Intake

Day __________Record item, time, and amount for everything you eat and drink for 3-7 days. Do you see a pattern?

Breakfast	
Lunch	
Dinner	
Snacks	
Water (oz)	
Beverages	
Other	

Analyze Your Intake

Items you are eating / drinking more of or less of than you expected:

More of ____

Less of ____

Amount of water you drank per day on average: _____ oz or _____ ml

Unless medically inadvisable, aim to drink half your weight in ounces of water each day. (If you weigh 128 pounds, drink 64 ounces of water or 2,000 milliliters.)

When you ate.

Typically most people are less active in the late afternoon and evening hours and most calories ingested during those hours go to one's waist.

On average did you eat most of your calories before five pm?

☐ No ☐ Yes

Other observations ____

____

____

Your plan to address problem areas related to intake ____________________

____

____

____

Example of GI and GL Table

Glycemic Index = GI Glycemic Load = GL **Type of Food (GI 55 or below = low)** **(GL 10 or below = low)**		**GI: Glucose= 100**	**Serving in grams (28 gms = 1 oz)**	**GL: Per serving**
Bread	Baguette, white, plain	95	30	15
	Kaiser Roll	73	30	12
	Pita bread, white	68	30	10
	Pita bread, whole wheat	57	64 (1 pita)	17
	Pumpernickel	56	30	7
	Sourdough, medium slice (not whole grain so limit to 1-2 slices a day)	53	37	6-8
	White bread, commercial yeast	71	30 (1 slice)	10
	Whole wheat, commercial yeast	71	30	9
Cereal	Puffed Wheat	80	30	17
	Bulgur Wheat	48	150	12
	Oatmeal, instant or quick	83	250	30
	Oatmeal, old fashioned	55	250	13
Drinks	Coca Cola®	63	250 mL	16
	Apple juice, unsweetened	44	250 mL	30
	Gatorade	78	250 mL	12
	Tomato juice, canned	38	250 mL	4
Grains	Barley, pearled (average)	28	150	12
	Popcorn, plain (average)	55	20	6
	Corn on the cob, sweet	60	150	20
	Quinoa	53	150	13
	Brown rice	50	150	16
	White rice	89	150	43
Fruits	Apple	39	120	6
	Banana, ripe	62	120	16
	Grapefruit / Orange	25 / 40	120 / 120	3 / 4
	Grapes	59	120	11
	Raisins	64	60	28

Glycemic Index = GI Glycemic Load = GL Type of Food (GI 55 or below = low) (GL 10 or below = low)	GI: Glucose= 100	Serving in grams (28 gms = 1 oz)	GL: Per serving
Legumes Black beans	30	150	7
Hummus (chickpea salad dip)	6	30	0
Kidney beans	29	150	7
Lentils	29	150	5
Navy beans	31	150	9
Peanuts, raw	7	50	1
Pinto beans	55	84 (3 oz)	57
Soy beans	15	150	1
Nuts Cashews, salted	27	50	3
Peanuts, raw or dry roasted	7	50	0-1
Dates Dried	42	60	18
Pasta Macaroni,	47	180	23
Macaroni and Cheese (Kraft)	64	180	32
Spaghetti, white, boiled	46	180	22
Spaghetti, whole-meal, boiled	42	180	17
Pizza Plain baked dough with parmesan cheese and tomato sauce	80	100	22
Spaghetti White, boiled, average	46	180	22
Whole wheat, boiled, average	42	180	17
Tortilla White flour (has added fat)	30	50	8
Tortilla Corn (no added fat)	52	50	12
Veggies Avocado	0	120	0
Green peas	51	80	4
Carrots	39-71	80	3-7
Baked potato, average	85	150	26
Mashed potato, average	92	150	18
New potatoes, average	57	150	12
Sweet potato / yam, average	70 / 54	150	22 / 20
Parsnips	52	80	4

Longevity Lifestyle—Sample Recipes

Breakfast in a Cup

After you get out of bed in the morning, drink a glass of water with a little lemon juice. When you want a change or are short of time, begin your day with breakfast in a glass.

You can make this nutrient-rich drink with mostly frozen ingredients, so they can always be readily available. You can also use the same recipe to replace dinner a couple times a week. In that case, you may want to leave out the nuts.

Ingredients

- 1 cup coconut water with no added sugar, or non-dairy milk
- ½ small banana
- ½ cup frozen berries, any type
- ¼ - ½ cup frozen kale
- ¼ cup frozen mango
- 1 Tbsp pea protein or hemp protein or other protein powder *
- 1 Tbsp Chia seeds
- 1 Tbsp raw nuts, if desired
- 4 ice cubes and another ¼ cup of coconut water or plain water as needed to achieve desired consistency

Preparation

Place ingredients in a blender and blend on high for 20-30 seconds. Blend again for another 20-30 second until very smooth.

Serving

Pour into a large cup or glass and feed your brain and body with superfood nutrients.

If not drinking all the shake immediately, you may need to stir it, otherwise the chia seeds may swell and sink to the bottom.

* Some prefer using pea protein rather than typical soy-based or dairy-based protein powders for a healthier drink. Pea protein provides more grams of protein per serving than hemp protein, although hemp contains more fiber.

A 2012 nutritional analysis published in Argo Food Industry Hi Tech reported that pea protein is nutritionally similar to casein and eggs.

A similar nutritional analysis published in 2010 in the Journal of Agricultural and Food Chemistry found that hemp protein is more nutritionally related to plant foods such as grains, nuts, and seeds.

References (Accessed Feb '15)

http://www.livestrong.com/article/544389-hemp-vs-pea-protein/

http://www.livestrong.com/article/249145-health-benefits-problems-of-soy-protein-powder/

Country Cornbread

Native Americans were using ground corn or maize for thousands of years before European explorers arrived in the New World. It was popular during the Civil War, too, because it was inexpensive and could be made in many different forms. Today, cornbread stuffing is associated with Thanksgiving holidays. This recipe is baked in a large cast-iron skillet. However, you can choose to use cast-iron fritters or mini-muffin tins or even a square casserole dish.

Ingredients

- 1 cup cornmeal *
- 1 cup all-purpose gluten-free flour
- 4 Tbsp baking powder
- ¼ cup sweetener (honey, maple syrup)
- 2 Tbsp olive oil
- 2 Tbsp unsweetened applesauce
- 2 Tbsp ground flax seeds
- 2 Tbsp Chia seeds
- 2 Tbsp egg replacer
- Scant ½ cup water
- ¾ tsp sea salt
- 1 cup non-dairy milk (almond, rice, coconut-almond)

Preparation

Spray a cast-iron frying pan with olive oil and place in oven. Turn oven on at 425 degrees F to preheat.

Place ground flax seeds in scant ½ cup of boiling water. Reduce heat and simmer for a few minutes until thickened, stirring periodically. (Alternatively, place scant ½ cup water and flax seeds in a blender and whiz until smooth. Place mixture in a saucepan, bring to a boil, then simmer for a few minutes until thickened, stirring periodically.) Set aside.

Place flour, cornmeal, baking powder, and salt in a bowl and mix well. Add sweetener, non-dairy milk, olive oil, and applesauce. Beat until smooth but avoid overbeating.

Carefully remove heated cast-iron frying pan from oven. Re-spray with olive oil as needed. Pour batter into frying pan and return to the oven. Bake for 20-25 minutes until edges are beginning to brown and a toothpick inserted in the middle comes out clean.

Remove from oven and place frying pan on a wire rack to cool for 10 minutes.

Serving

Cut into 8 or 10 wedges (depending on size of frying pan) and remove using a cake turner. You can invert the cornbread uncut onto a breadboard, turn right-side up and slice, if preferred.

Goes well with Black Bean Chili, Curried Lentil Pottage, Split Pea Soup, and/or salad.

Variations

To make corn spoon bread, follow recipe, adding one small can diced Ortega Green Chilies and one cup of frozen baby white corn (thawed). When baked, place cast iron skillet on the table and serve with a large spoon.

* Cornmeal is simply dried corn that has been ground into powder. A 3.5 ounce serving contains 10 grams of protein and 9.4 grams of fiber, plus a variety of micronutrients including antioxidant phytonutrients.

References (Accessed Feb '15)

http://www.livestrong.com/article/262936-what-are-the-benefits-of-eating-corn-meal/

http://www.whfoods.com/genpage.php?tname=foodspice&dbid=90

Broccoli Cranberry Salad

Raw broccoli makes an unbelievably good salad. Packed with phytochemicals and antioxidants, it is sometimes referred to as a powerhouse of nutrients. Reported to benefit the cardiovascular system and the immune system, and to have anti-inflammatory and even cancer-preventing properties, this vegetable is fat free and low in sodium and calories. What with the cranberries, raisins, and seeds, it hardly seems like *just broccoli.*

Ingredients

- 2 cups finely chopped raw broccoli (heads and soft parts of peeled stems)
- ¼ cup dried cranberries (soak in warm water for 30 minutes and chop)
- ¼ cup golden raisins (soak in warm water for 30 minutes and chop)
- ¼ cup sunflower seeds
- ¼ pecans, chopped

Preparation

Place all ingredients in a large bowl and mix well.

Add 4 ounces of Lemon Poppy Seed Dressing (free of high fructose corn syrup and hydrogenated fats), or use your own favorite.

Mix well.

Refrigerate overnight. Goes well with almost any entrée or soup.

Serving

Divide onto four portions, place on salad plates and serve.

Energizer Salad

Eat like a Prince for lunch—or at an early dinner if you are doing two meals a day. Fresh, raw veggies and fruits make a good combination for a fresh salad loaded with micronutrients. This salad is a winning combination of flavors, colors, and textures. Many grocery stores now have pre-washed and read-to-eat packages of baby spinach. Although this recipe calls for dried black figs, you can substitute fresh figs if they are available and you enjoy them.

Ingredients

- 1 standard package baby spinach leaves (washed and ready to use)
- ½ to 1 cup dried black figs, sliced very thin (about 8 figs)
- 1 cup strawberries, washed and sliced
- ½ cup pecans, halves or pieces
- ½ cup lite poppy-seed dressing or lite balsamic vinaigrette (free of preservatives and artificial coloring)

Preparation

Combine ingredients in a large bowl and mix gently.

Pour dressing over ingredients and mix gently to lightly coat the ingredients.

Serving

Place serving bowl on the table and allow individuals to help themselves or divide and serve on salad plates.

Serves six as a side salad and three to four as a main course.

Pasta 'n Kale

More and more people are realizing the benefits of Kale. English settlers are credited with bringing Kale to the new world in the seventeenth century. This is a 'complete meal' dish that combines fresh kale with pasta.

Unique and delicious, it is easy to prepare the dressing ahead, along with the oranges, putting each in a separate little bag or dish in the refrigerator. Likely there won't be any left over to save for another meal!

Ingredients

- 1 pound raw kale (I like cut and pre-washed in a package)
- 10 oz angel hair pasta or spaghetti (I prefer rice or a non-wheat mix)
- ½ cup almonds, sliced
- ½ cup peanuts, dry roasted
- 2 navel oranges
- ½ cup dried cranberries

- Dressing:

  3 Tbsp Chinese chili sauce or equivalent
  2 tsp honey or agave nectar or equivalent
  2 tsp unseasoned rice vinegar or Kiwi vinegar
  2 -4 tsp orange zest (to taste)
  1 tsp soy sauce or Bragg's amino acids (or more to taste)
  1 tsp minced or crushed garlic
  ¼ heaping tsp unrefined sea salt
  ½ tsp lemon pepper or pepper (to taste)
  ¼ c. olive oil

Preparation

If you use pre-cut pre-washed kale, pull or cut out large stem pieces and discard before placing kale in the colander. Otherwise, wash kale and cut out the large stems. Roll kale leaves into a tight roll and cut in ½ inch slices with a sharp knife. Place in a colander and set aside.

Mix dressing ingredients in small bowl. Peel oranges and cut into small pieces.

Cook pasta according to package directions (I break pasta into three or four lengths as it makes it easier to eat with the kale.)

When cooked, **pour pasta PLUS pasta water into colander over the kale.** Let drain for several minutes.

Pour drained pasta and kale into a large shallow bowl. Lift and mix with tongs.

Pour in dressing and add almonds, cranberries, peanuts, and orange pieces. Lift and mix with tongs.

Serving

Use tongs to serve portions onto each plate as a main dish.

* Kale, a green leafy vegetable, is a member of the Brassica family, which includes Brussels sprouts, collards, and cabbage. Kale is packed with nutrition, providing iron, potassium, calcium, and trace minerals; vitamin K, and some of the B vitamins. Although low in calories (one cup contains only 34 calories), kale contains 2.2 grams of protein, 1/3 grams of fiber, and 121 milligrams of omega-3 fatty acids.

References (Accessed Feb '15)

http://www.livestrong.com/article/250505-kale-nutrition-information/

Peanut Sauce

They're called 'peanuts' but this nutritious item is a legume and not a true nut. Yes, it's good with fresh veggie rolls but also with other things, too: dribbled over salads or steamed broccoli or cauliflower or baked potatoes (instead of butter and sour cream). Some like the taste of peanut sauce better when it is made with dry roasted peanuts (rather than old fashioned peanut butter out of the jar) or with powdered peanut butter, which has eighty-five percent less fat calories.

Ingredients

- 1 cup raw or dry-roasted (unsalted) peanuts or ½ cup powdered peanut butter *
- 3/4 cup non-dairy milk (almond, coconut-almond) Note: May substitute 1 package Mori Nu silken tofu for liquid, if desired.
- 1 Tbsp Tamari (gluten-free) soy sauce
- ½ tsp cayenne pepper or red pepper flakes (or more to taste)
- 1 clove garlic (or ½ tsp garlic powder)
- ¼ tsp sea salt
- 1 tsp honey or other sweetener
- 1 tsp lemon or lime juice (if you want a less sweet taste)

Preparation

Place nuts in a blender and whiz until powdery. [Note: If using powdered peanut butter, just place all ingredients in the blender at one time.]

Add all other ingredients and whiz until smooth. You may need to stop and scrape down sides with a spatula.

Check consistency. Sauce should be quite thin and pour easily. Add more non-dairy milk or some water as needed, a teaspoon at a time, to achieve desired consistency.

Serving

Use as a dip for celery or jicama sticks or dribble a tablespoon or so over steamed veggies or baked potato.

Peanuts are quite nutritious but also relatively high in fat, so use a small amount of peanut sauce as a delicious condiment—for flavor.

Note: Store unused sauce in the refrigerator (tightly covered container) for 7-10 days or freeze. When thawed, stir well and add more water or non-dairy milk, a teaspoon at a time as needed, to obtain desired consistency.

* Relatively low on the Glycemic Index, an ounce of dry-roasted peanuts contains 164 calories, 6.6 grams of protein, 6 grams of carbohydrates, including 2.2 grams of fiber, and 13.9 grams of fat, including 1.9 grams of saturated fat. Estimates are that raw or dry-roasted peanuts contain 19 percent of the daily value for niacin and 9-11 percent of the daily value of Vitamin E.

References (Accessed Feb '15)

http://www.livestrong.com/article/489676-what-is-healthier-dry-roasted-or-regular-peanuts/

http://www.whfoods.com/genpage.php?tname=foodspice&dbid=101

Black Bean Chili

Chili can be enjoyed on the patio or in the park during summer months and around the fireplace or family dinner table in the winter. It's a nutritious and feel-good dish, chunky and chewy. By adding a bit of Basmati brown rice to the beans you get a perfect protein.

The grated carrot adds vitamins and a dash of color and texture without overwhelming the dish. Cilantro, an herb native to Mediterranean regions and Turkey, makes a great garnish topping.

Ingredients

- ¼ cup Basmati brown rice
- 1 cup water
- ¼ tsp Himalayan salt
- 1 medium white onion, chopped quite fine
- 1 carrot, grated
- 2 cloves minced garlic
- 1 cup celery, cut crosswise into thin slides
- 2 15-oz cans black beans, rinsed well and drained *
- 1 cup water
- 4 Roma tomatoes, diced
- 2 Tbsp nutritional yeast (not Brewer's yeast)
- 1 Tbsp chili powder
- 1 Tbsp McKay's chicken-style seasoning or equivalent
- ½ tsp Himalayan salt
- ¼ cup cilantro **
- ¼ tsp pepper

Preparation

Bring 1 cup water and ¼ tsp Himalayan salt to a boil.

Add Basmati brown rice. Return to a boil, then turn down heat and simmer until rice is soft and all liquid is absorbed stirring periodically until rice is fluffy and soft. May add small amounts of additional water, if needed.

While rice is cooking, spray a frying pan with olive oil and place over medium heat. Add chopped onion, garlic, grated carrot, and celery. Cook until onion begins to soften, stirring constantly. Remove from heat.

Place 1 cup water and 2 cups black beans in blender and pulse until quite smooth. Pour into a large saucepan.

Add all remaining ingredients and bring to a boil, stirring constantly. Turn heat down and simmer slowly for 20-30 minutes, stirring periodically to keep from sticking. When cooked to your taste, remove from heat.

Serving

Ladle into soup bowls or cups. Garnish with cilantro.

Can also be served over oven-roasted cubes of sourdough bread.

* Black beans are considered a low-calorie dense food, which makes them more filling. They contain nutrients found in protein foods such as poultry and seafood, as well as nutrients found in vegetables such as spinach and broccoli. A ½ cup serving of cooked black beans contains 8 grams of protein and less than 1 gram of fat.

** Cilantro is a popular Mediterranean herb. Both leaves and seed can be used in cooking. This herb is filled with phytonutrients. One of the richest herbal sources for ***Vitamin K***, Cilantro also contains minerals such as potassium, calcium, manganese, iron, and magnesium.

References (Accessed Nov '14)

http://www.whfoods.com/genpage.php?tname=foodspice&dbid=2

http://www.nutrition-and-you.com/cilantro.html

Garlic Potato Casserole

Many cultures use potatoes extensively in their cuisine in many different forms using a variety of recipes that often differ by culture. Scalloped potatoes is often cited as a favorite. However, many typical ingredients are high on the Glycemic Index and Glycemic Load listings.

This non-dairy recipe is lower on GI and GL lists and still tastes fabulous. Instead of white, use a mix of gold, red, and even purple potatoes. *

Ingredients

- 8 cups of scrubbed (or peeled) potatoes cut into 1/8th inch slices
- 3 medium white onions, chopped
- 6 cloves garlic minced or 2-3 tsp prepared minced garlic
- 1½ cups water
- 2 cups non-dairy milk (e.g., almond milk)
- ¾ cup raw cashews
- 1 Tbsp mock chicken-style seasoning or equivalent
- 1 tsp olive oil
- ¾ tsp Himalayan salt
- ½ tsp pepper
- ½ cup sourdough breadcrumbs or Panko Japanese style breadcrumbs

Preparation

Place raw cashews in a blender with water, almond milk, and seasonings. Set aside to soak while preparing potatoes and onions.

Place olive oil in frying pan over medium heat. Add minced garlic and cook until softened. Add chopped onions. Sprinkle with salt and ground pepper to taste. Sauté until soft. Remove from heat and set aside.

Spray a 9 x 13 glass casserole with olive oil. Layer half the sliced potatoes evenly over the bottom of the casserole.

Distribute the onions evenly over the potatoes. Layer the remaining sliced potatoes on top.

In blender, whiz the cashew-water-milk-seasonings until very smooth. Pour over the potato-onion mixture.

Sprinkle breadcrumbs over the top.

Place covered casserole in oven preheated to 450° F. Immediately turn oven heat down to 350° and bake for 30 minutes. Remove cover and continue to bake for another 30-40 minutes until edges are starting to brown and potatoes are thoroughly cooked.

Remove from oven and allow to sit on a rack for 5 minutes.

Serving

Cut into squares. Lift out with a pancake turner and place a serving on each plate. If you use a large spoon be sure to spoon out all three layers in each serving.

* Purple potatoes, native to South America, can be used like regular potatoes. They are especially rich in antioxidants. A serving of three small purple potatoes has 131 calories, no fat or cholesterol, 3 grams of protein, and 4 grams of dietary fiber.

References (Accessed 10/14)

http://www.livestrong.com/article/346316-purple-potatoes-nutrition-facts/

Crispy Cookies

Chia seeds come from a desert plant known as *Salvia hispanica*, dating back to Mayan and Aztec cultures. The word chia means strength, and legend has it that these ancient cultures used the tiny seeds as an energy booster.

An unprocessed, whole-grain food, chia seeds contain healthy omega-3 fatty acids, protein, carbs, fiber, antioxidants, and calcium. The outer layer of chia seeds swells when mixed with liquids to form a gel.

Ingredients

- 2½ cups old fashioned oatmeal (uncooked)
- 3 bananas, mashed
- 1 tsp coconut oil
- ½ cup Chia seeds
- 1 cup applesauce
- ¼ cup non-dairy milk (almond, rice, coconut)
- ¼ cup grated coconut
- ½ cup raisins (rinse in hot water and drained)
- ½ cup chopped nuts
- ½ cup dried cranberries
- ½ cup finely diced dried figs or dates
- 1 Tbsp real maple syrup
- 1½ tsp cinnamon
- 2 tsp vanilla

Preparation

Place Chia seeds, mashed bananas, non-dairy milk, applesauce, cinnamon, coconut oil, and vanilla in a small bowl and mix well. Set aside.

Place oatmeal, raisins, nuts, coconut, and dried fruit in a mixing bowl and stir well. Add Chia seed mixture and stir well.

Using a metal ¼ cup measure, fill and tap out onto a cookie sheet that has been sprayed with olive oil. Flatten each slightly into about a 2-inch diameter size.

Place in oven preheated to 375° F. Reduce heat to 350° F.

Bake for 20-25 minutes until brown and crispy.

Serving

Remove from oven. Let cool and serve.

They freeze well, if there are any left.

Use for dessert, in place of a muffin at breakfast, or as a snack on a hike or at the beach.

References (Accessed 8/14)

http://healthyeating.sfgate.com/top-10-health-benefits-chia-seeds-6962.html

http://www.doctoroz.com/blog/lindsey-duncan-nd-cn/chia-ancient-super-secret

http://www.webmd.com/diet/features/truth-about-chia

Additional recipes and other resources are available at:

www.LongevityLifestyleMatters.com

www.LLM.life

www.SharletBriggs.com

www.ArleneTaylor.org

The body is like a piano, and happiness is like music—it is needful to have the instrument in good order.

—Henry Ward Beecher (1813 – 1887)

Resources

- *Your Brain Has a Bent (Not a Dent)* 3rd Edition (paperback, eBook, audiobook); coauthored with W. Eugene Brewer, EdD

- *Beyond the House of Silence* (paperback, eBook, audiobook in process), coauthored with Marilyn Banford, PhD

- *Brain Benders*—brain aerobic exercises (paperback)

Aging Series – Coauthored with Sharlet M. Briggs, PhD

- *Age-Proofing Your Brain—21 Factors You Can Control,* 2nd Edition (paperback, eBook, audiobook)

- *Age-Proofing Your Memory: Scripture* (paperback, eBook)

- *Age-Proofing Your Memory: Ultimate* (paperback, eBook)

- *Age-Proofing Your Memory: Mormon* (paperback)

- *Age-Proofing Your Memory: Catholic* (paperback)

Longevity Lifestyle Matters – with Steve Horton M.Div., MPH, and Sharlet M. Briggs, PhD

- *Longevity Lifestyle Matters*—paperback, eBook, audiobook)

- *LLM—Companion Notebook* (paperback, eBook)

  Available in English and in Spanish

Adventures Series – Coauthored with Sharlet M. Briggs, PhD

- *Adventures of Aimi* (paperback, eBook, audiobook)
- *Adventures of Stella* (paperback, eBook, audiobook)
- *Adventures of Buddy-the-Beagle* (in process)
- *Adventures of the Longevity Mystery Club* (paperback, eBook, audiobook)

Chronicles Series

- *Chronicles of the Alabaster Owl* (paperback, eBook, audiobook in process)
- *Chronicles of the Littlest Dolphin* (paperback, eBook, audiobook in process)
- *Chronicles of the Jungle King* (paperback, eBook, audiobook in process)

Paperbacks, eBook, and audiobooks are available from and distributed by:

www.PacificHealth.org/store/

Paperbacks and some DVDs are available at: www.amazon.com

'You only get one brain and one body to last your entire lifetime. Your health rarely improves by chance—it can improve by incremental positive change and your recommended preventive maintenance program is a Longevity Lifestyle.'

—Arlene R. Taylor

Arlene R. Taylor, PhD, a leading speaker on brain function, is sometimes referred to as the *brain guru.* She specializes in simplifying this complex topic so individuals can more easily grasp and implement practical strategies that can help them thrive. A sought-after speaker, she has spoken to thousands internationally. A member of the National Speakers Association, Taylor is listed with the Professional Speakers Bureau International.

Taylor is founder and president of Realizations Inc, a non-profit corporation that engages in brain function research and provides related educational resources. She has a Master's in Epidemiology and Health Education, and two earned doctorates.

Taylor has worked with health and wellness programs for decades, including the McDougall Program, Smoke Free Life, the Brain Program, selected 12-Step programs, addiction programs, and Grief Recovery groups.

She believes that your brain-body health is the best investment you can make and that creating and maintaining a brain-based *Longevity Lifestyle* not only begins in the brain but also is key to success.

Contact Dr. Taylor through - www.ArleneTaylor.org

'With appropriate motivation, education, practical application, and the right use of their brains, individuals may feel better, look better, think more clearly, and live healthier lives—longer.'

—Steve Horton

Steve Horton M.Div., MPH, is interested in and enthusiastic about health and wellness, believing that a *Longevity Lifestyle* not only is possible but also can be effective and enjoyable. Even fun.

His goal is to provide educational resources in a stimulating, easy-to understand, and practical-to-apply format. When implemented as part of a life-time commitment, the information and strategies can help people in the community become more aware of simple lifestyle changes they can make to benefit their overall health, avoid preventable diseases, and reduce symptoms associated with chronic illnesses to the extent possible.

Horton has two earned Master's degrees and is completing a doctoral program.

Horton is CEO of Pacific Health Education Center (PHEC), headquartered in Bakersfield, California. PHEC exists to promote health, disease prevention, and an enhanced understanding of brain function through education--internationally.

Horton and his wife, Dr. Kimberly Horton, who holds a senior executive position for a healthcare system, make their home in Northern California.

Contact Horton at – stehor123@sbcglobal.net

'Everything begins in your brain. That includes your health. Use your brain to create and maintain a Longevity Lifestyle—because it matters.'

—Sharlet M. Briggs

Sharlet M. Briggs, PhD, has been interested in brain function and its impact on communication and behaviors for over a quarter of a century. Emerging research from brain-imaging studies has opened a new window into organizational performance. She uses her expertise in community presentations, facilitating business groups, providing seminars and workshops, and counseling leaders.

Having been affiliated with healthcare for most of her career, she understands the challenges, roadblocks, and opportunities faced by business leaders in the challenging arena of healthcare.

Passionate about the positive contributions that brain-function information can make when practically applied personally and professionally, Briggs speaks internationally.

Briggs has a Master's in Counseling and an earned doctorate in Clinical Psychology. She is Market President and Chief Executive Officer for Kern County, California, including Adventist Health Bakersfield and Adventist Health Tehachapi Valley.

Briggs and her husband, David O. Eastman, who has a background in administration for a healthcare network, make their home in California.

Contact Dr. Briggs through - www.thrivingbrain.com

Ultimately, the things which most affect the quality of your life are your decision.

—Ralph Marston

the
End